AUTHORS GUIDE

Book Publishing for the Rest of Us!™

"You have a wonderful team. You are giving publishing back to the authors, without whom there would be no books. Keep up the good work!"

— **George Denniston, MD, author**

Publisher Bruce Batchelor, shown here with our mascot Tyhee, self-published his first book way back in 1975 – over twenty years before Trafford invented on-demand publishing and made self-publishing so much more affordable, convenient and efficient for authors around the world.

TRAFFORD

Trafford on-demand publishing service™ was created *by* self-publishing authors *for* self-publishing authors to fill a market gap. Since mid-1995, we've been refining and expanding our service package, and proving the concept works with authors from over forty countries (over 3000 titles) and book sales into over four dozen countries (so far). More authors are joining every day. On-demand publishing fits perfectly with today's work and life styles – it allows modern authors to efficiently publicize and retail their books on a global scale without leaving their neighbourhood.

© 1998, 1999, 2000, 2001, 2002, 2003 Trafford Holdings Ltd. All rights reserved. No part of this publication may be reproduced, stored in a retrieval system, or transmitted, in any form or by any means, electronic, mechanical, photocopying, recording, or otherwise, without the written prior permission of the publisher.

Written by Bruce Batchelor, design and illustrations by Marsha Batchelor.

*NOTE: this guide was printed on 20# bond paper with a 10 pt Carolina card cover (not laminated) and perfect binding on the same equipment that will be used to print **your** book on-demand in response to orders from around the world. The trim size is 7.5 inches (wide) by 10.75 inches (tall). Fonts used include Times 10/14 for most body copy, plus Helvetica, Lucida Sans, Helvetica Black and Ribbon (for the script-style words in the headlines).*

Canadian Cataloguing in Publication Data
Batchelor, Bruce T., 1950-
   Authors guide
   ISBN 1-55212-206-9
   1. Self-publishing. I. Batchelor, Marsha
   R. (Marsha Ruth), 1952- II. Title.
Z285.5.B37 1998   070.5'93   C98-910302-1

TRAFFORD on-demand publishing service™

Suite 6E, 2333 Government St., Victoria, BC, Canada V8T 4P4
Phone 250-383-6864   Toll-free 1-888-232-4444 (Canada & US)
Fax 250-383-6804   Email info@trafford.com
Website www.trafford.com
Trafford catalogue # 96-0101   www.trafford.com/robots/96-0101.html

   Prospective authors from the Eastern USA may contact our North Carolina office:
   Trafford Publishing Inc., Attn: Carol Reed, 301 South Front Street, Suite #8
   New Bern, NC 28560-2105 coreed@trafford.com 1-888-240-3723 fax 252-633-4816

   With offices also in Drogheda, County Louth, Republic of Ireland & Crewe, Cheshire, UK

25   24   23   22   21   20   19-E-V

This Authors Guide is dedicated to future generations of authors

Art work above by Daniel Batchelor, age 6

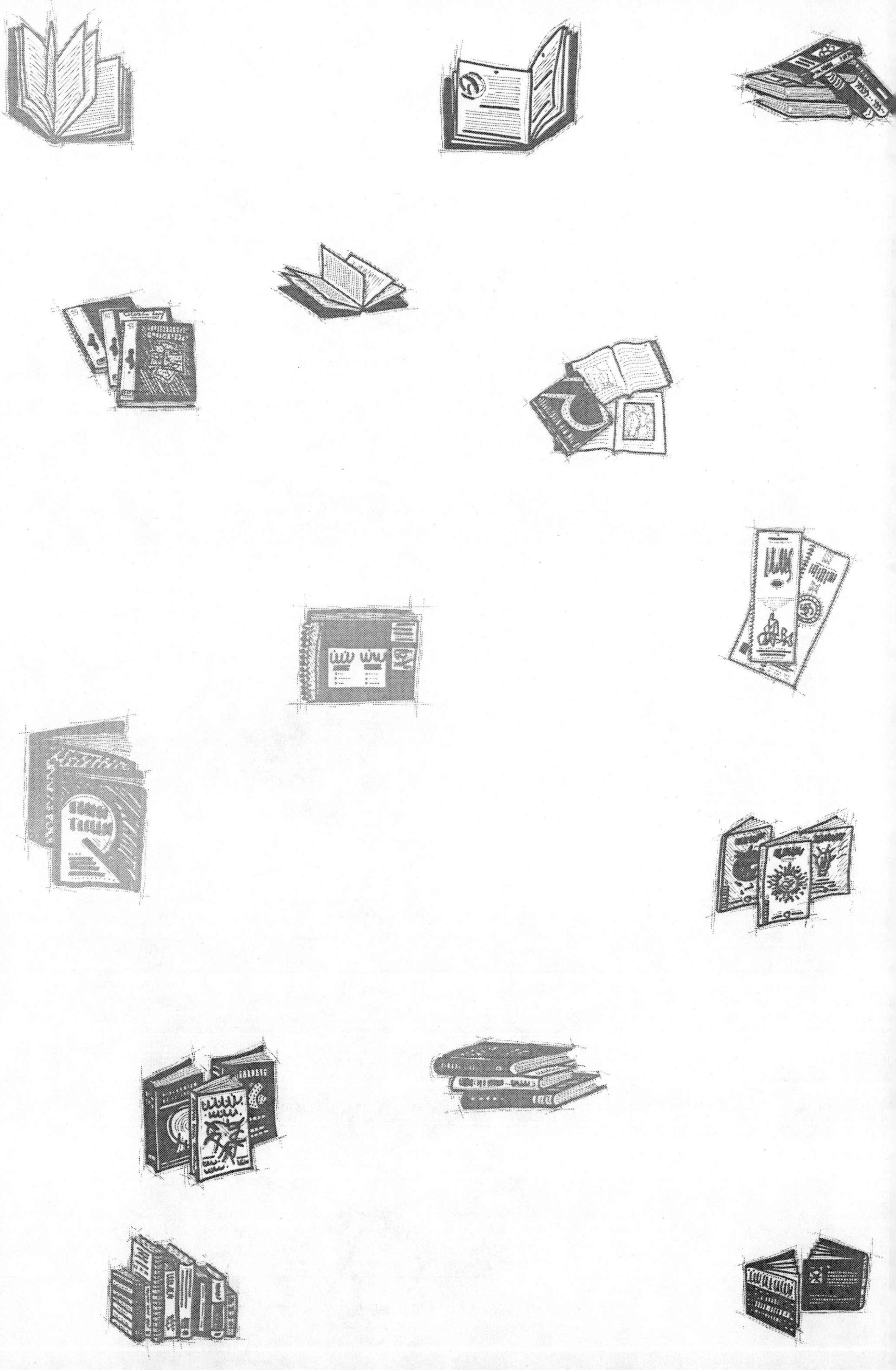

CONTENTS

Welcome to on-demand publishing, a robust service for your book

Book publishing for the rest of us: affordable and convenient	7
Experiencing success	8
Select what you need	9
Publishing Steps: a brief overview of what's in Trafford's on-demand publishing package	10
ISBN	13
CIP data, Library of Congress number and Dewey Decimal coding	14
Copyright and legal deposit	15
EAN and UPC barcodes for bookstores and other retailers	16
Receiving royalties	17
Personal use copies	18
Announcement of your book's availability	19
Web page	20
Notifying search engines	21
Creating hyperlinks	22
Announcement cards and colour postcards	23
Access for buyers through Trafford's bookstore	24
Selling at key bookstores	25
Authors' orders	26
Print-on-demand production	27
Perfect binding and full-colour cover	28
Prompt order fulfilment	29
Physical appearance	30
Changes and updates	32
Copyright and agreement	33
Movie rights and other sales	34
Price and royalty	35
Accessing book professionals	36
Selling an e-book version	37
Questions and answers	39
Technical specs	47
Author checklist	53
Metadata form	54
Contract	57
Chart of printing costs and minimum retail prices	62

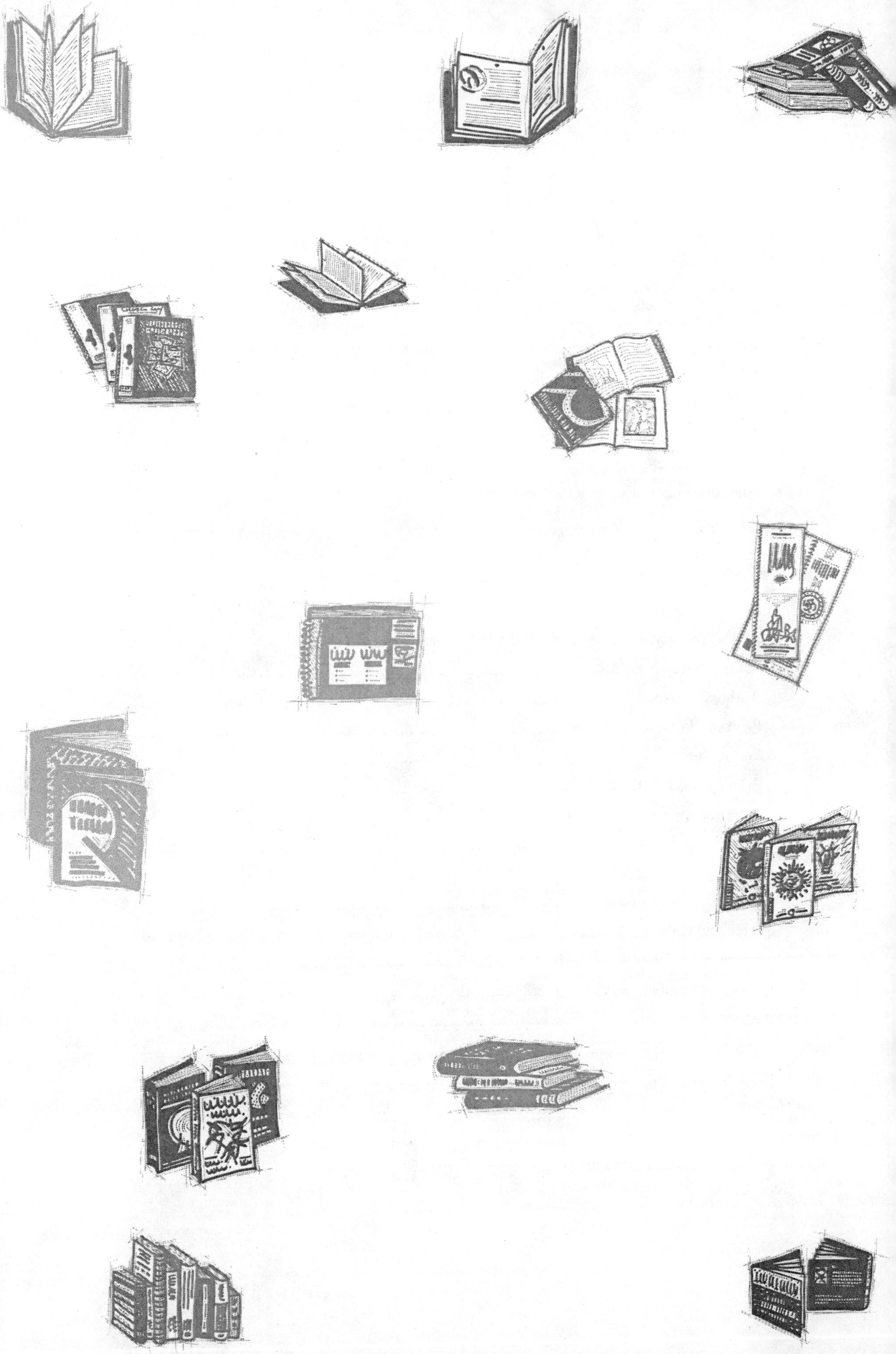

AFFORDABLE AND CONVENIENT

Book publishing for the rest of us!

Have you written a book, training materials or how-to guide that others might want to buy? Consider an amazing service created *by* self-publishing authors *for* self-publishing authors – the innovative Trafford on-demand publishing service™. For US$990 (CDN$1490), your book will be published and available for purchase by bookbuyers around the world. We call this the "Best Seller Package." Another offering, the "Entrepreneur Package" priced at US$679 (CDN$969), is designed for those who opt to handle all the publicity and distribution themselves, but still want the advantages of on-demand printing and Internet order fulfilment. The "Legacy Package," valued at US$499 (CDN$699), assists the author with publishing's legal and administrative aspects, and with preparing a perfect-bound book with a full-colour cover.

On-demand publishing is a practical combination of conventional publishing tasks, print-on-demand manufacturing and Internet marketing and retailing. Trafford handles publishing's legal and administrative requirements, helps with publicity and manages the retail sales. Whichever package is chosen, the author retains copyright, sets the retail price, decides on design and appearance, and directs publicity work. Using print-on-demand equipment, complete books are manufactured one-at-a-time to fill incoming orders – which means the self-publishing author *need not make a large investment in preprinted books stored in a warehouse.* Selling directly to the customer over the Internet is very cost-effective and opens a global market for your book.

Sound great? After investigating the alternatives, you'll be even more impressed with how affordable, convenient and comprehensive Trafford on-demand publishing service™ really is!

Press clipping

"... [With Trafford's service] self-publishers [can] get that novel or manual into many more hands than they could shake in a lifetime, and with smaller initial financial risk."
—Capital News, *Kelowna, BC*

Measures of Success

Ann Marie Parisi's book *Lunch Bag Notes* is a collection of inspirational messages her father wrote on her school lunch bags. Parisi's book is meant to bridge the 'silence gap' between teens and their parents.

EXPERIENCING SUCCESS

Each self-publishing author defines success in his or her own way

Measures of success

Every self-publishing author has his or her own definition of success – we know this from asking those currently using this service (they come from over forty countries so far). Here's a peek at what's gratifying for some Trafford authors…

- The Minneapolis-St. Paul *Star-Tribune* said retired investment broker Tom Morison's satire, *Pounce*, "has a fable-like quality, is very well written, thoroughly engaging and deserves a wide audience." Tom was in Morocco writing a second book when he sent a postcard saying, "I'm having more fun at this 'work' than I've ever had in my life."
- Ernie Palamarak is writing a series of 'Rune Erikson' adventure novels, each set in a different exotic locale – his holidays double as "research trips."
- Dennis Lockwood-Lee wrote *A Letter To Lawrence* for his son describing Dennis's lifelong search for life's meaning.
- One of Trafford's first titles, *1984: The Ultimate Van Halen Trivia Book* by Lucas Aykroyd, is being promoted on many fan websites. The group's manager told Lucas that the band members thoroughly enjoyed reading it. Then Lucas was invited to meet his idols backstage.
- We've scattered many other examples throughout this guide…

Will your self-publishing project be financially lucrative?

Whether a book is self-published using Trafford on-demand publishing service™ or is released by a major book publisher, no one can accurately predict or guarantee sales levels. Trafford's service considerably reduces a self-publishing author's financial investment (largely by eliminating the need for an inventory of preprinted books), provides efficient global sales channels, and handles many publicity and administrative functions. The author is encouraged to generate additional publicity, through whatever means available, to ensure potential buyers are aware of the book. The retail price and corresponding royalty per book are set by the author, based on his or her assessment of the book's audience. Ultimately, however, it is the bookbuying public who will determine the number of copies sold. Some books generate a trickle of sales; by contrast, one author set a royalty record in February 2001, earning over $9,300 (over $14,700 Cdn) in one month!

> **Measures of success**
>
> Betty Eckgren's A Changed Man *tells the fascinating tale of how her father assumed a new identity during WWI – and only told his wife and daughter his real name when near death. Betty invites readers to help solve the mystery of why he did it.*

Some authors treat our service as the "minor leagues" of publishing – an opportunity to develop and prove one's craft. For others, simply seeing their writing in print and for sale fulfills a lifelong dream. On-demand publishing provides a new process and cost-effective opportunity for publishing your book; it is really up to the individual author personally to define what will constitute a successful book publishing experience.

What's your motivation?

SELECT WHAT YOU NEED

Three great packages to help you attain your writing goals

	Legacy Package **(L)**	Entrepreneur Package **(E)**	Best Seller Package **(B)**
CORE LEGAL, ADMIN. AND ODP SERVICES			
Assign an ISBN number	Included	Included	Included
Obtain CIP data listing, LoC number & Dewey coding	Included	Included	Included
Insert copyright page information into manuscript	Included	Included	Included
Create EAN and UPC barcodes for the back cover	Included	Included	Included
Print directly from author's PostScript file or scan author's 'print-ready' pages into a PostScript format	Included	Included	Included
Do cover layout - includes 2 hours of work	Included	Included	Included
Full-colour cover (lamination optional extra cost)	Included	Included	Included
Perfect binding	Included	Included	Included
Print, bind, trim and mail 1 proof copy	Included	Included	Included
Print two copies and deposit at National Library	Included	Included	Included
Store (and backup) print files for book and cover	Included	Included	Included
Print copies of book to fill author's orders, with no minimum run length, and discounts for larger runs	Included	Included	Included
TRAFFORD BOOKSTORE SERVICES			
Create webpage with photos, author bio, excerpts, etc.	--	Included	Included
Set up author's book in inventory/pricing file	--	Included	Included
Accept orders through Trafford.com bookstore	--	Included	Included
Process charge card payments through Trafford.com	--	Included	Included
Invoice and ship books to fill Trafford.com orders	--	Included	Included
Pay quarterly royalties on Trafford.com sales	--	Included	Included
PROMOTION AND DISTRIBUTION SERVICES			
Submit for sales at Amazon, Borders.com, Barnes & Noble	--	--	Included
Submit for sale at Chapters.Indigo.ca web site in Canada	--	--	Included
Submit book to Bowker's Books-In-Print & BookData UK	--	--	Included
Announce your book's launch to industry & media contacts	--	--	Included
Inform key search engines about the book's webpage	--	--	Included
Provide 250 announcement cards & 100 colour postcards	--	--	Included
Process orders from libraries, booksellers & distributors	--	--	Included
Deliver 10 copies of book to author for mailing to reviewers	--	--	Included
Pay author quarterly royalties on all sales	--	--	Included
REMOTE ON-DEMAND PRINTING AND E-BOOKS			
NEW! – Sell book via Internet download (PDF format)	--	--	Included*
* some technical restrictions apply			
Price in US Dollars (Canadian Dollars)	$499 ($699)	$679 ($969)	$990 ($1,490)

OPTIONAL EXTRAS

Transcribing from typewritten manuscript or out-of-print edition into digital form .... ask for quote
Layout of inside pages – for standard novels and memoirs (ask for details) .... US$500 (Cdn$750)
Author's Alterations (AAs) – revisions after you've submitted your book ..... US$48/hour (Cdn$70/hour)
Additional proofs including printing, binding, packaging & airmail .... US$15 (Cdn$25) each
Cover design and alterations (beyond the 2 hours included in all packages) ... US$48/hour (Cdn$70/hour)
Laminated covers, other bindings, thicker paper, colour pages ...... see Printing Costs on pages 62 and 63

PUBLISHING STEPS
Your book deserves a comprehensive publishing service

The service is quite efficient: your book could be published and publicized in four to six weeks.

You've devoted considerable time and resources to writing your book. Now, as a self-publishing author, you can feel confident that your book will receive the attention it deserves by taking advantage of the comprehensive **Trafford on-demand publishing service**.™ Here is a brief overview of what's in the publishing packages available from Trafford. (**L**, **E** and **B** indicate the benefits included in the Legacy, Entrepreneur and Best Seller packages respectively.)

Trafford handles publishing's administrative and legal requirements
- a unique International Standard Book Number (ISBN) allows customers and publishing industry workers to locate and order your book quickly *(see details on page 13)* **L**, **E** and **B**
- cataloguing-in-publication (CIP) data, Library of Congress number and Dewey Decimal coding provide the globally-recognized indexing required for libraries *(see page 14)* **L**, **E** and **B**
- copyright notice is included and two dated copies are deposited with the National Library *(see page 15)* **L**, **E** and **B**
- barcodes meets bookstores' and other retailers' scanning requirements *(see page 16)* **L**, **E** and **B**
- earn royalties on the very first copy sold – we send cheques quarterly *(see page 17)* **E** and **B**

Book production and order fulfilment take advantage of on-demand printing
- print-on-demand manufacturing means no investment for preprinted books stored in a warehouse, and no waste from unwanted or outdated books (that's totally environmentally correct!) *(see page 27)* **L**, **E** and **B**
- we'll prepare a print-on-demand master file from your digital file or by scanning your print-ready originals *(see page 27)* **L**, **E** and **B**
- we'll prepare a full-colour cover based on your design and artwork *(see page 28)* **L**, **E** and **B**
- you receive ten bound copies for reviewers and/or your personal use *(see page 18)* **B**
- books are printed, bound and shipped generally within 3 to 5 business days of a customer's order being received, so your title need never become 'out-of-print' or 'back-ordered' *(see page 29)* **E** and **B**
- you can order copies at special "author order" rates for your own distribution* *(see page 26)* **L**, **E** and **B** (* *pay for the exact number of copies you need, when you need them – allow up to three weeks for printing large quantities*)

The author controls all key factors
- you determine the book's physical appearance, including page layout, cover style (from basic to full-colour), binding (spiral or perfect bound/paperback), trim size and other characteristics *(see page 30)* **L**, **E** and **B**
- you can make changes or updates at any time by revising the master file *(see page 32)* **L**, **E** and **B**
- you retain full copyright and may end the agreement at any time *(see page 33)* **L**, **E** and **B**
- you keep all rights for translations, foreign sales, movie rights and serialization, and are encouraged to pursue any distribution opportunities you wish *(see page 34)* **L**, **E** and **B**
- you set the retail price, which determines the royalty amount *(see page 35)* **L**, **E** and **B**

Cost-effective, global sales channels make your book easily purchased
- your book will be available through Trafford's Internet bookstore and can be ordered by toll-free phone, fax, website, email or regular post *(see page 24)* **E** and **B**
- it will also be submitted for sales through some of the world's largest on-line bookstores and distribution companies *(see page 25)* **B**
- NEW! – your book could be available to be purchased as an e-book (digital download) *(some technical restrictions apply; see page 37)* **B**

Together, we'll get the word out to potential buyers
- an announcement is emailed to thousands of book industry and media contacts, and information is sent to key industry reference services *(see page 19)* **B**
- potential readers can evaluate your book at its own web page, which features a description, cover image, sample excerpt, author's biography blurb and photo *(see page 20)* **E** and **B**
- they can quickly locate that web page through key search engines *(see page 21)* **B**
- we provide the HTML code for placing hyperlinks to your book's web page at other web locations *(see page 22)* **E** and **B**
- you receive 250 printed publishing announcements to hand out and 100 colour postcards featuring your book's cover *(see page 23)* **B**

You have access to book publishing professionals
- professional book services, including editing, ghostwriting, proofreading, illustration, book design, layout and extended publicity work, may be accessed – at the author's discretion and expense – through Trafford's website, if not available in your community *(see page 36)* **L**, **E** and **B**

Trafford on-demand publishing service™—practical, comprehensive publishing packages for surprisingly affordable prices

These publishing steps
(process, benefits and responsibilities)
are explained in detail on pages 13 through 37

Please note: on-demand produced books can be attractive, practical and durable. They look like most other softcover books and manuals in bookstores. The process, however, is not suitable for book designs that require glossy pages, many colour pages, high resolution photographs, embossing, die-cutting or hardcovers (casebound).

NEWS: we have an amazing new service for authors and illustrators of short, full-colour books – such as kids' picture books. Please ask for the guide *"Have You Written a Kids' Book?"* which explains this breakthrough in colour book publishing affordability, simplicity and efficiency.

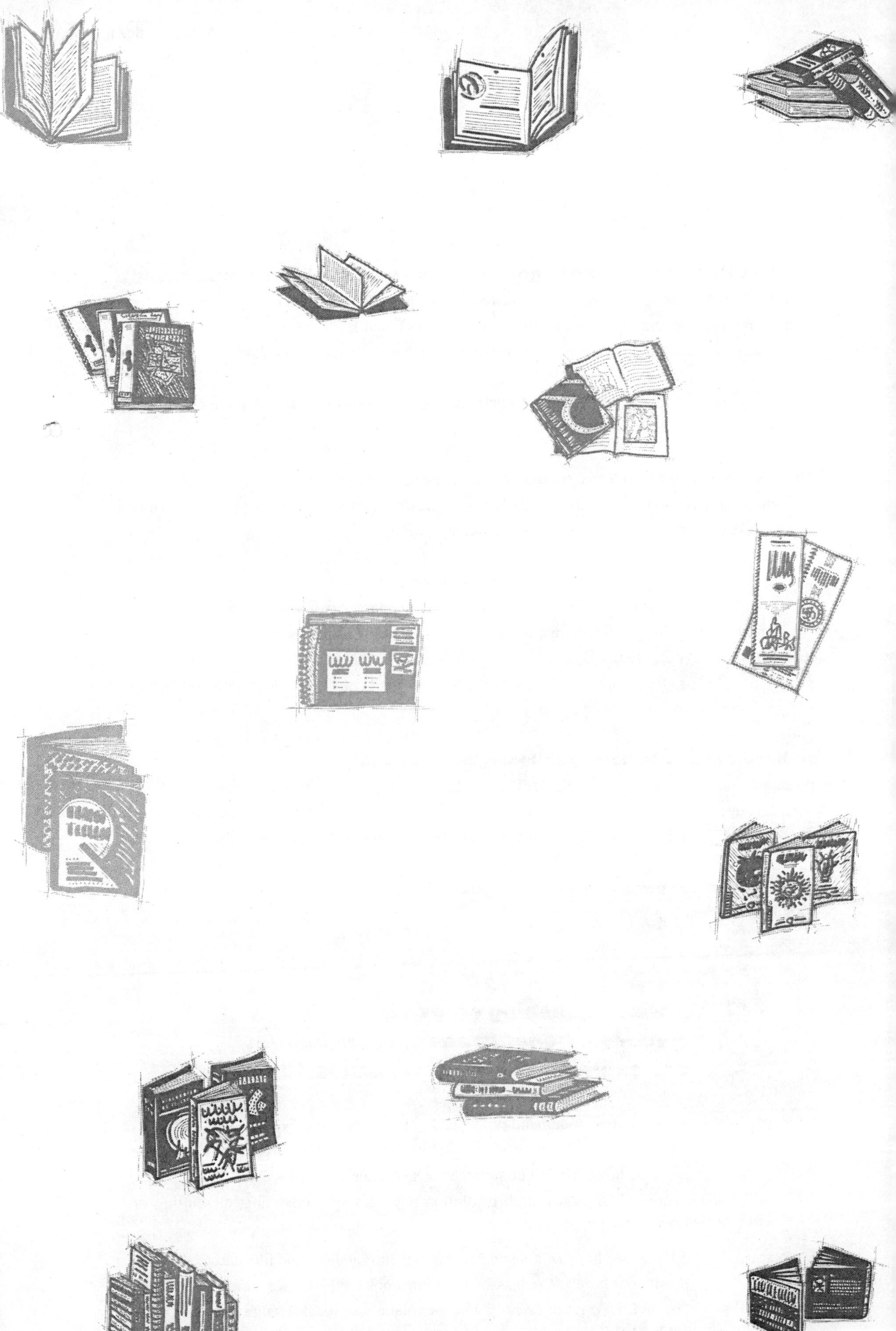

ISBN
Process, benefits and responsibilities

Benefit: a unique ISBN enables bookstores and libraries worldwide to locate and order your book quickly *(included in all three packages).*

Explanation

The ISBN (International Standard Book Number) system uniquely identifies all books published worldwide. All parts of the book trade use these identification numbers for inventory control, ordering and accounting. About a million ISBNs are assigned each year for English-language publications alone.

An ISBN is a unique and unchangeable number, identifying one title (specifically one binding or edition of the title) published by one publisher. An example of a Trafford-assigned ISBN is 1-55212-000-7 which identifies *Yukon Channel Charts*. The first six digits identify the publisher as Trafford. The next three digits (000 in this example) uniquely identify *Yukon Channel Charts* within one of the blocks of ISBNs allotted to Trafford. The final digit (7) is a mathematical check digit. Because all publishers' contact information is kept current at common reference sources, such as Bowker's Books-In-Print and BookData UK's databases, bookstores and librarians worldwide can determine quickly where to purchase a copy. The ISBN identifies a "publisher," rather than the author, since people in the book trade expect to order from the publisher. Although you are "self-publishing" using our service, the book trade considers Trafford as the "publisher" for ISBN purposes.

Larrein Trudeau's Spirit Knows *is a disarmingly honest account of the path from abuse to wholeness*

Press clipping

"Trafford... has used the Internet to create a new type of business, one that adds value and reduces cost. And is friendly to the environment as well. The idea here is that the Internet is not a solution in itself, just another tool that can be used by business creatively to put products, services and customers together."

—in 'The Net as Business Tool: Rewards Will Go to Innovators' by Sid Tafler

Trafford's role and responsibilities

Trafford staff will immediately assign an ISBN to your book when you sign on. We'll use that ISBN to identify work dockets, for generating barcodes and a host of other activities.

Author's role and responsibilities

Please include your new ISBN with all communications to facilitate proper identification of your publishing project.

CIP DATA
Process, benefits and responsibilities

Benefit: cataloguing-in-publication (CIP) data, Library of Congress number and Dewey Decimal coding provide the globally-recognized indexing required by libraries and researchers *(included in all three packages).*

Explanation
The CIP system is fairly standardized and recognized around the world. It has been organized by national libraries to provide a single, consistent mechanism around the world for creating all books' classification information (and for researchers to search for specific items). Think of the drawers of small file cards that are still used in many libraries – the information on those cards is part of the CIP data. By having a central system and by printing a portion of the CIP data inside the book, the cataloguing information used at all libraries is similar. CIP information in databases are accessible to libraries in various on-line formats and on CD-ROM, so researchers can locate books published anywhere, including your book published by Trafford.

Only a portion of the full CIP record is printed inside the book. An example is shown below:

```
National Library of Canada Cataloguing in Publication Data
Batchelor, Bruce T., 1950-
   Yukon channel charts
ISBN 1-55212-000-7
F1095.Y9B3 1996      917.19'1043      C96-910403-0
```

In the last row, the first number is a **U.S. Library of Congress number** (used by academic libraries), the second is a **Dewey Decimal System** number (used by most public libraries), and the last is the Canadiana record number (for internal use at the National Library). Creating CIP entries is the job of a specialized group of professional librarians called cataloguers. They follow a thick book of protocol and curious conventions in determining the correct wording. For example, only the first word of the title is capitalized in the CIP entry, except for proper nouns. As well, a subtitle is not shown on the short CIP listing, although it is included in the complete record. Trafford currently registers all books through the Canadian library system because our main editorial offices are in Victoria, BC, Canada – your book's cataloguing information becomes available shortly afterwards to booksellers and librarians around the globe.

Trafford's role and responsibilities
Trafford staff will submit to a professional cataloguer the required information on the author and book. Once the entry that will appear in the book is returned, we will ensure it appears on the copyright page and also on the book's web page.

Author's role and responsibilities
The author must provide his or her full name (and the way the name is to appear on the cover, if different). Also we'll need your complete date of birth – this is so the cataloguer can distinguish between similarly-named people born in the same year. The country of citizenship is required as well. If there are co-authors or illustrators, their names, birthdates and nationalities will be required. Please completely fill out the Metadata Form on page 54.

COPYRIGHT AND LEGAL DEPOSIT
Process, benefits and responsibilities

Benefit: a copyright notice is included and two dated copies deposited with the National Library *(included in all three packages).*

Explanation

Generally, under US and Canadian laws, the writer automatically has copyright to his or her work from the moment it is written. US and Canadian copyright is recognized in most developed countries. However, this copyright can be lost or at least substantially weakened if you allow the material to be circulated without a copyright notice and especially if the material is circulated without charge. Freely circulated material that bears no copyright notice is generally considered to be "in the public domain." Having a dated copy on file at a national library could help if there is a dispute about copyright. Another important protection is the inclusion within the book of a copyright statement asserting that, for example: "© copyright 2003 by J. Francis Smith." Generally this statement appears on the reverse side of the title page along with the CIP data and Trafford's contact information. You may expand this with a statement similar to the following:

"All rights reserved. No part of this publication may be reproduced, stored in a retrieval system, or transmitted, in any form or by any means, electronic, mechanical, photocopying, recording, or otherwise, without the written prior permission of the author. Contact the author at...."

If you wish, you can write "Contact the author in care of Trafford Publishing" and we'll forward any correspondence.

Publishers in Canada (where Trafford's head office is) are required by law to deposit two copies of every new book with our National Library. If an author wishes to also send a copy to another government's copyright office, he or she is welcome to do so.

Trafford's role and responsibilities
Trafford staff will produce and send two copies to the National Library.

Author's role and responsibilities
The author guarantees, when signing the publishing agreement with Trafford, that he or she has clear copyright to all the contents, and that the material is free of illegal material (slanderous, libelous, likely to be deemed hate literature, pornographic, inciting unlawful activities, etc.).

When preparing the book layout, the author should, at minimum, include a basic copyright statement on the reverse of the title page. A longer all-rights-reserved statement is also recommended.

Measures of success

David Menashe and the NetReds Manchester United fan club assembled The World Wide Web of United, *a collection of sports anecdotes gleaned from the web. Profits are going to an English children's charity.*

BARCODES FOR BOOKSTORES
Process, benefits and responsibilities

Benefit: barcodes meet bookstores' and other retailers' scanning requirements *(included in all three packages).*

Explanation

Barcode scanners are now commonplace at retail checkout counters. As well, inventory and production quality controls rely heavily on identifying items by barcode.

Within the book industry, there is a special type of barcode, which complies with the Bookland EAN/ISBN standard (it is different from the ubiquitous UPC standard). This is the format we comply with when creating a barcode for each book's cover and one of the inside page. If you plan on having your book sold through local bookstores, this barcode will be needed.

If the author is certain of the retail price and confident that price will never change, the barcode can have a price suffix – extra bars on the right to code a retail price in one currency. Most of our books do not show a price.

Other retailers use the UPC (Universal Product Code) barcode. Because sales **not** in bookstores constitute more than half of all book sales, having a UPC barcode on your book's cover can be important in your marketing.

The top image is an EAN ISBN barcode used by bookstores. The lower image is a UPC barcode used by most other retailers.

Trafford's role and responsibilities

Trafford staff will generate the barcodes and place them on the cover and one of the inside pages.

Author's role and responsibilities

The author is encouraged to approach local and specialty bookstores and other retailers to urge them to sell the book.

Measures of success

Nancy Maynard, former owner of the Oakland Tribune and board member of National Public Radio in the US, wrote Mega Media *to stimulate discussion about how new media dynamics will impact news journalism.*

Nancy Maynard

RECEIVING ROYALTIES
Process, benefits and responsibilities

Benefit: earn royalties with the very first copy sold *(included in Entrepreneur and Best Seller packages).*

Explanation
Royalties are paid quarterly and include all royalties accrued during that period. Remember that, since we are producing books one-at-a-time to fill incoming orders from customers, the author doesn't have to pay for book manufacturing after investing in the initial on-demand publishing package – the author simply receives royalties on every copy sold, every three months. Incidentally, because of their arrangements allowing booksellers to return unsold copies, trade publishers pay royalties much less frequently and generally for a period that ends three or six months previously.

Authors can look up their books' on-going sales and royalty information on a confidential web page. As well, this information is included with the quarterly statements that are sent by mail.

A Canadian author will also be paid a Goods & Services Tax (GST) amount on royalties if he or she is a GST-collecting business or self-employed individual. Royalties to authors residing outside Canada will be paid in United States dollars. Authors may elect to have their royalties deposited directly into their Visa, MasterCard or Amex account.

Trafford's role and responsibilities
Trafford records royalties accruing to the author on each sale and sends a statement and cheque (or makes direct deposit) five weeks after the end of each calendar quarter.

Author's role and responsibilities
A Canadian author will advise Trafford if GST is payable on royalties, and provide the GST number. Please advise us if you'd prefer direct deposit of royalties into your credit card account, rather than a cheque.

Measures of success

Writer Ken Conibear's wife gave him a unique surprise 93rd birthday gift: republishing two of his books from the 1930s and publishing a manuscript that had been sitting 'in the closet' since the late 1940s. Ken was dubbed the "Kipling of the North" before WWII by reviewers of his bestselling books about life in Canada's north.

PERSONAL USE COPIES
Process, benefits and responsibilities

Benefit: receive ten copies for reviewers or personal use *(included in Best Seller package).*

Explanation
Included in the Best Seller publishing package is the production of twelve copies. The law stipulates that two of these must be deposited with the National Library – the other ten are mailed to the author to send to reviewers or for other uses.

Trafford's role and responsibilities
Trafford produces twelve copies. Trafford staff will deposit two copies, on the author's behalf, with the National Library. Trafford staff will send ten copies to the author.

Author's role and responsibilities
None, except to decide who is going to receive a complimentary copy of your printed book.

Carolyn Fleming from Florida used characters, settings and experiences from her own childhood in the Deep South when writing her delightful period novel Journey Proud.

Press clipping

"For unknown writers, Trafford's service is an inexpensive route to self-publish their books.... Trafford's focus on niche markets is also worth noting. Even though the Web is a global market, we suspect there are many regional and speciality opportunities for services that deliver books on demand through the Internet."
—The Seybold Report on Internet Publishing

ANNOUNCING YOUR NEW BOOK
Process, benefits and responsibilities

Benefit: an announcement is emailed to thousands of book industry and media contacts, and information is sent to key industry reference services *(included in the Best Seller package).*

Explanation
Once your book is ready for sale, we'll send an announcement via email to a list of thousands of book industry and media contacts. The wording used is the book's "teaser" or brief description taken from the metadata (see page 54) submitted by the author.

At the same time, Trafford staff will submit information on your book to key industry reference databases: BookManager/PubStock, Books-in-Print, BookData UK, Froogle.com and others. These services are used by bookstores and libraries to track down the availability of books when filling customers' special requests. We are continually expanding the number of services we notify – Froogle.com is the latest.

Trafford's role and responsibilities
Trafford staff will distribute an announcement via email to industry and media contacts, using text provided by the author in the metadata form. We will also notify key industry reference services.

Author's role and responsibilities
The author will create the descriptions to be used in announcing your book. The brief description (maximum 30 words) will be included in the email announcement sent to thousands of industry and media contacts. The same brief description and the full description will be sent to key reference services within a few weeks of the launch.

The author is encouraged to send out news releases to local media and otherwise publicize the availability of your book. **DO NOT send an unsolicited announcement to a broad list of email addresses!** Such unwelcomed mail is called *spam* in the Internet world and can elicit extremely hostile reactions, including a shutdown of Trafford's server.

WEB PAGE
Process, benefits and responsibilities

Benefit: potential readers can evaluate your book at its own web page, which features a description, cover image, sample excerpt, author's biography and photo *(included in the Entrepreneur and Best Seller packages).*

Explanation
Our experience has shown that potential readers want to know more about a book than simply the title and author's name. Before they will buy, most want to go through the on-line equivalent of reading the book's dustjacket and scanning a few inside pages. We enable them to browse through a description of the book (provided by the author), see the front cover, know more about the author (and see a photo if the author so wishes), and even read the table of contents or a sample excerpt. Sometimes the author chooses the introduction or foreword as the sample. If the book has been favourably reviewed, portions of the review can also be included on the web page.

Each book's web page has its own unique, permanent Internet address [URL] of the form www.trafford.com/robots/00-0002.html. The web pages are actually generated (and updated nightly) by our proprietary ODP™ software from database fields, so there is no mechanism for authors to design their own pages. If you have web designing talent, we urge you to create additional web pages promoting your book at other locations and include hyperlinks to refer potential buyers to the book's URL at Trafford's server where that all-important purchase can occur.

Trafford's role and responsibilities
Trafford staff will ensure that the necessary information is submitted by the author, that the cover and author's photo are scanned, and that all data are entered appropriately into the ODP™ database. In addition to the descriptions and sample excerpt, some of the items that readers will be able to see are: number of pages, cost, type of binding, name of co-publisher (if there is one), ISBN, CIP data and comments from favourable reviews that are brought to our attention.

Author's role and responsibilities
The author writes a brief description (one or two sentences) plus a longer description (typically two or three paragraphs), selects an excerpt to display, provides a biographical blurb "about the author" and has the option to include a "mug shot." As well, the author submits a list of up to 12 keywords that potential readers would likely use to track down this type of book. (See author's checklist on page 53 and metadata form on page 54 for a complete rundown on the information needed. Where possible, please paste the information into an email message to your author services rep at Trafford, identifying it clearly by ISBN.)

Once the web page has been created, the author needs to proofread it carefully. Then tell us okay (or nay) by email, with details of any corrections required. If the author isn't equipped to proofread on the Internet, Trafford staff can fax or mail you a paper printout.

NOTIFYING SEARCH ENGINES
Process, benefits and responsibilities

Benefit: potential readers can locate your book quickly through Internet search engines *(included in the Best Seller package)*.

Explanation
People searching for information on the Internet generally enter keywords at search engine sites, such as Altavista, Lycos, Google, Yahoo and others. Search engines (technically, some are *search directories*) use software programs called *knowbots*, *worms* or *spiders* that roam tirelessly around the Internet, reading through web pages and indexing all the contents. When a knowbot finds hyperlinks on a web page, it will read through all those pages too, fanning out and on and on. With billions of web pages to chew through, it could take ages before your book's new web page is included. To help expedite the process, we inform key search engines about your book's new page.

These index-creating knowbots are especially intrigued by keywords they'll find in the *meta tags* hidden in your page. The keywords are taken from the metadata form you fill out to tell us about your book. We reinforce this emphasis on the right keywords by specifically including them in our notifications to the search engines.

Trafford's role and responsibilities
Trafford staff will ensure that key search engine sites are promptly informed of new web pages. Depending on the workload at those sites, it may take a few weeks before search engines can direct their knowbots to read your book's web page. Our current submission list includes Altavista, Lycos, Google, Yahoo, MSN, HotBot, Overture and AlltheWeb. Other search engines will search these popular search engines, so within a few months the information is available at all major reference sites.

Author's role and responsibilities
The author provides all the information (with particular attention to those keywords on htge metadata form) necessary for the creation of the web page.

Measures of success

Walt Taylor's Waging Peace for a Living
is a blueprint for worldwide change.
It was favourably reviewed in the Washington Post

CREATING HYPERLINKS
Process, benefits and responsibilities

Benefit: to increase awareness, you can place hyperlinks to your book's web page at other web locations *(included in the Entrepreneur and Best Seller packages).*

Explanation
Your book's web page is located on Trafford's web server. We'll tell you the page's unique address [URL] so you can pass on this URL to friends, businesses and others who have websites related to your book's topic or genre. Ask them to set hyperlinks to your book's URL. We will provide the HTML computer code for such a hyperlink, but if you are not familiar with how to solicit or create hyperlinks, we suggest you enlist a friend or find a student to help. The value of these links cannot be overemphasized: people can't buy your book unless they are aware of it.

Webmasters at most sites are generally more than cooperative about placing links to web pages (such as your book's) that could interest their readership – it increases their site's utility as a comprehensive referral spot. A site dedicated to your book's niche interest, whether it is model trains or a particular rock band, is the ideal spot to solicit a prominent hyperlink to your book's web page. A personal request (and thank you) from the author is often sufficient, although some authors send a complimentary book to the site's editor as a courtesy. On occasion, this "freebie" copy sparks a favourable review and a "link of the week" spotlight – and exposure to hundreds or thousands of prime bookbuying candidates.

As mentioned before, if you have web design talent, we urge you to create web pages promoting your book at other locations, possibly with more information on you or your organization, and then refer potential buyers to the book's Trafford URL to complete the transaction. Many Internet service providers offer free web pages – check out where you access your email. The more awareness you can generate, the better.

Some authors have participated in chat room sessions and subscribed to newsgroup lists to talk up their book, mentioning the URL. Many authors also include the URL in their email 'signature' which appears at the bottom of all their outgoing correspondence.

Trafford's role and responsibilities
Trafford staff will provide the author with the book's web page address [URL], and provide the HTML code for inserting a hyperlink into an existing web page at another location.

The code will be similar to the following, with your book's catalogue number replacing the `00-0001` in this example:

```
Read more about my book at<A HREF="http://www.trafford.com/robots/00-0001.html">www.trafford.com/robots/00-0001.html</A>.
```

Author's role and responsibilities
The author is strongly encouraged to publicize the book by attempting to have hyperlinks placed as widely (and well-targeted) as possible across the Internet. Remember not to send unsolicited emails (spam)!

CARDS & COLOUR POSTCARDS
Process, benefits and responsibilities

Benefit: you receive 250 publishing announcement card to pass out and 100 colour postcards featuring your book's cover *(included in the Best Seller package)*.

Explanation
The author usually comes into personal contact with many potential buyers: friends, business associates, relatives, fellow hobbyists, neighbours, local librarians and others. Trafford provides a supply of announcement cards (business-card size) which have the basic information required to order your new book. Since many people are still not using the Internet, the cards list the handy toll-free phone and fax numbers, plus Trafford's mailing address.

We also provide 100 colour postcards showing your book's cover.

This new book is available from Trafford

When In Doubt, Follow The Yellow Brick Road
by Bernard J. Srode

TRAFFORD
Suite 6E, 2333 Government St., Victoria, BC, Canada V8T 4P4
Phone 250-383-6864   Fax 250-383-6804
Toll-free 1-888-232-4444 (Canada & US only)
Order at www.trafford.com/robots/00-0123.html
ISBN 1-55212-458-4

The business-card size announcements are great for passing out at readings or other personal appearances. The colour postcards can be included in press kits or other correspondence, or sent on their own.

Trafford's role and responsibilities
Trafford staff will print announcement cards and postcards and ship them to the author. Extras may be ordered in lots of 250 cards or 100 postcards for US$25 or CDN$35 (includes mailing).

Author's role and responsibilities
The author is strongly encouraged to publicize the book at all possible personal appearances, giving out these announcement cards to provide potential buyers with ordering information. Mailing out the postcards to your network of friends and associates can spread awareness quickly and jump-start sales.

Canadian Sherry Irvine (above) and Nora Hickey of Ireland created a book using the Internet to send and review draft versions

Measures of success

Nora Hickey and Sherry Irvine's Going to Ireland *received great reviews and sells briskly at their genealogy seminars across North America and Europe.*

ACCESS FOR BUYERS
Process, benefits and responsibilities

Benefit: your book will be available at Trafford's bookstore (via the Internet web, toll-free phone, fax, email or regular post) *(included in the Entrepreneur and Best Seller packages)* **and can be ordered through other bookstores** *(Best Seller package only)*.

Explanation

Your book will be available for purchase on-line at Trafford's bookstore at www.trafford.com (this is **not** included in the Legacy package).

For customers not using the Internet, our Trafford bookstore has a toll-free phone number, fax and regular mailing address. For those titles published under a Best Seller package only, bookstores can locate your book through its ISBN and place orders directly with Trafford for their customers.

To supplement the distribution channels mentioned above, the author (all three publishing packages) has the option to purchase a quantity of books at the low print shop price (see page 26) to set up local distribution through bookstores and personal appearances.

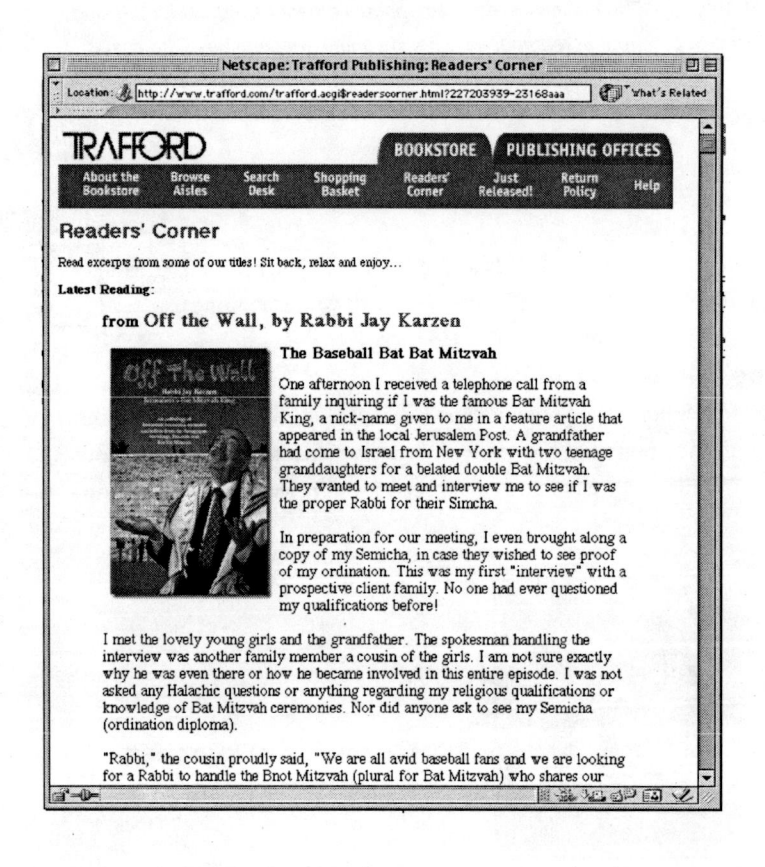

Trafford's role and responsibilities

Trafford staff will ensure that the book is available through Trafford's on-line store and via phone, fax and mail.

Author's role and responsibilities

The author is encouraged to supplement these distribution methods by purchasing low-cost "author order" copies and organizing other sales initiatives.

SELLING AT KEY BOOKSTORES
Process, benefits and responsibilities

Benefit: your book will be available at some of the world's most visited on-line bookstores *(included in the Best Seller package).*

Explanation
We list our books with Baker & Taylor (one of the world's largest book distributors) and various reference sources. Your book will also be submitted to three or more high-traffic websites. Currently our latest books are being listed at bn.com (Barnes & Noble's website), Chapters.Indigo.ca (Canada's largest book chain), Amazon.com, BookSense.com and Borders.com.

Because of the state-of-flux at the large e-retailers, listings may take weeks or even months to appear, the list of retailers may change, and individual retailers may change how they list titles. (We can't control how retailers conduct their business.) Changes or corrections may also take weeks to happen. Customers may find your book by browsing aisles, but most sales will come from people looking specifically for your book at a site with which they are familiar and comfortable making a purchase.

Barnes & Noble's distribution center now stocks a few copies of almost all Trafford titles so they can show "in stock" availability at bn.com. We cannot, however, *guarantee* B&N will stock your book. At most other retailers, such as Amazon.com, the reality is that order processing and procurement of not-in-stock titles may take these vendors 3 weeks or more. The fastest order fulfilment will always be for orders customers place directly at the www.trafford.com bookstore (that is also where the author earns the highest royalty).

Trafford's role and responsibilities
Trafford staff will submit information about your book to at least three high-traffic on-line vendors and one major distributor.

Author's role and responsibilities
Help generate awareness/interest/desire/action so people will buy books through these distribution channels.

AUTHORS' ORDERS
Process, benefits and responsibilities

Benefit: you can order copies at special "author order" rates (minimum 60% off retail price), in any quantity *(included in all three packages).*

Explanation

When the physical characteristics of your book (such as page count, covers, binding, size, etc.) are finalized, Trafford will calculate a single-copy printing cost. The charts near the back of this guide show how the cost is determined, and the volume discounts. You can order books for local bookstore sales and other distribution at this price (or less, depending on quantity) with no minimum quantity. There is a US$10 ($15 CDN) admin/handling/packaging charge on any author order of less than 50 books.

If you are planning to sell through local bookstores, be aware that about 40% discount off retail is sought by these merchants (distributors require 50% to 55%). The author may wish to order at least 50 copies at a time to take advantage of the discounts off the single-copy printing price and to minimize shipping costs.

If you wish to order thousands of copies (which we don't recommend until you've thoroughly experimented at the short-run, on-demand level and proven the market demand for your book), ask us to obtain a quote on your behalf from one of our printing suppliers. We have good relationships with some of North America's largest book printing companies, and can secure excellent prices for you.

Under the North American Free Trade Agreement (NAFTA) there is no customs duty on books, though a broker's fee may be levied at the border on large orders.

Trafford's role and responsibilities

Trafford will promptly fill "author orders," granting discounts with larger orders. See pages 62 and 63 for discounts.

Author's role and responsibilities

The author may order copies at the single-copy printing price or better. There is no minimum quantity. Please be aware that printing of orders of 500+ copies may take up to two weeks. When planning, allow time also for shipping from our Victoria, BC, Canada location.

Press clippings

"On-demand publishing is an invitation to self-publishing authors [whose books] may not fit into the conventional mold of publishing because of a narrow audience or unusual subject matter.... The initial set-up cost [is] a fraction of the investment which would otherwise be required to self-publish.... Trafford offers organizations, corporations and governments an opportunity to... divest themselves from publishing obligations and expenses."
—Print On Demand Business Canada

PRINT-ON-DEMAND PRODUCTION
Process, benefits and responsibilities

Benefit: print-on-demand manufacturing means no investment for preprinted books stored in a warehouse, and no waste from unwanted or outdated books *(included in all three packages)*.

Explanation

Relatively recent technological advances make it possible for Trafford to produce a single bound book in response to each incoming order. Both the covers and the 'book block' (the inside pages) can be manufactured using this 'print-on-demand' equipment.

The on-demand publishing approach pioneered by Trafford saves the self-publishing author what might otherwise be a considerable investment in printing and storage of books. Since books are printed only *after* an order is received and payment verified, it is the *bookbuyer* who pays for the printing when it occurs, not the author.

In on-demand publishing, the author provides a 'print-ready' original. This contrasts sharply with conventional trade publishing practices, in which the author relinquishes all control, and the design is created – and paid for – by the publishing house.

You'll want a satisfactory design and layout – satisfactory to yourself and, of course, also satisfactory for enticing people to purchase a copy. If a specific visual appearance is critical to your vision of the book, and you aren't experienced with book design, some consulting time with an experienced graphic designer may be in order. You can find someone in your local community by asking for a referral at a local print shop, or look on Trafford's talent pool bulletin board. Trafford's staff can also provide layout service on a limited number of book projects. A competent graphic designer should be able to create a print-ready original which is crisp and handsome – satisfactory to all and in keeping with the author's vision for the book.

Please see page 47 for technical specifications.

Trafford's role and responsibilities

Trafford staff will assist the author (and/or the graphic designer) in understanding the range of possibilities and technical requirements. Once the 'originals' have been submitted, best efforts (a maximum of two hours of a technician's time for the inside pages and two more for the cover) will be made to create a workable print-on-demand master file, either by scanning your 'originals' or printing your digital file, or a combination of both. If unforeseen difficulties do arise with the originals, the author will be notified before any surcharges are incurred.

Trafford staff will produce a bound proof copy that will be sent for the author's review before any retail copies are sold.

Author's role and responsibilities

The author is responsible for ensuring a satisfactory design or layout of the book. You can submit the 'originals' as either paper printouts or a digital PostScript file, or a combination of both. On receipt of the proof copy, you will promptly notify Trafford of your approval or any concerns.

PERFECT BINDING & FULL-COLOUR COVER
Process, benefits and responsibilities

Benefit: looking good because people do judge a book by its cover (included in all three packages)!

Explanation

On-demand printed books, if well designed and well manufactured, can hold their own on any bookseller's racks. An author often devotes years to creating the manuscript (we know the investment in time and emotion because many of our staff are writers themselves), and definitely wants the end result to be a "real book." Although there are options to have simpler covers and a variety of spiral and wire bindings, our authors generally choose a full-colour cover and a perfect binding. Perfect binding is the trade name for a "paperback" book's glued binding.

The covers are produced on a digital toner-based laser printer on card stock. The output from any laser printer is not completely consistent from day to day. There will be subtle variations in tone and intensity, most noticeably with pastels and other light colours. Lamination is optional at an additional cost (for perfect bound books of 100 pages or more). This lamination process is not ideal: although they are more durable, laminated covers may curl noticeably as humidity levels change.

Our talented technical staff will devote two hours to creating an attractive cover layout for your book, working from your files and artwork. If you are sending artwork, please ensure you have unrestricted rights to use those images from the creators.

Trafford's role and responsibilities

Trafford's staff will produce a colour cover layout, working from the author's files and artwork.

Author's role and responsibilities

The author is responsible for submitting a digital cover layout with all required artwork or, at minimum, sketches of what's desired on front and back and all necessary materials (photographs for scanning, illustration originals, text for the back cover, etc.). Technical specifications start on page 47. The author is responsible for carefully reviewing and approving the proof.

Athlete/author Chris Lear

Measures of success

Sportswriter Chris Lear chose to test market his book, Running with the Buffaloes, *using Trafford's system. The book quickly became one of Trafford's top sellers as Chris promoted the book relentlessly, and word-of-mouth recommendations were spread by athletes around the world. Within five months of its Trafford launch, Chris was offered a lucrative contract by New York-based The Lyons Press for a hardcover edition and national promotion.*

PROMPT ORDER FULFILMENT
Process, benefits and responsibilities

Benefit: books are printed, bound and shipped generally within 3 to 5 business days *(included in the Entrepreneur and Best Seller packages).*

Explanation
Out-of-print? Never! Because of our print-on-demand system, orders are filled promptly, without worries of being out-of-print or back-ordered. We strive to fill and ship most retail orders within 5 business days – many orders actually go out the next day after an order is received. Note that retail order taking is *not* included within the Legacy publishing package. Legacy authors may, of course, order books at any time for themselves.

Trafford's role and responsibilities
Trafford aims to fill and ship all retail book orders within 5 business days. Large orders from the author may take longer, as we need to reserve a block of time for the print run.

Author's role and responsibilities
Help generate interest so there are lots of orders to fill!

Measures of success

After retiring, Judith Petres-Balogh and her husband moved to Hungary and found themselves leading an intriguing life. This Old House by the Lake *describes their triumphs and tribulations as they adjusted to a different culture.*

PHYSICAL APPEARANCE
Process, benefits and responsibilities

Benefit: the author determines the book's physical appearance, including page layout, cover style (from basic to full-colour), binding (perfect bound, spiral, plus other choices), size and other characteristics *(included in all three packages).*

Explanation
Trafford's service begins with a print-ready original – the author is responsible for design and layout (typesetting) of the book, deciding on the physical appearance within the bounds of our manufacturing capabilities. A first-time author is advised to study previously published books at a bookstore or library to clarify the 'vision' for his or her book, as there are an infinite number of design possibilities. If a specific visual appearance is critical to your vision, and you aren't experienced with book production, some consulting time with an experienced graphic designer may be in order. You might find someone in your community (ask for a recommendation at a local print shop), or look on Trafford's talent pool bulletin board at www.trafford.com/4dcgi/Talent.html. As well, check to see if our own staff have available time to lay out your book. Expect layout to involve at least 10 to 15 hours of a technician's time, priced at US$48 per hour (CDN$70). A novel can be fairly straightforward to lay out, whereas a how-to manual full of photos, graphs, charts and tabular work will require many days of concentrated effort.

Appearance
On-demand produced books can be attractive, practical and durable. They can look like most other softcover books and manuals in bookstores. The process, however, is not suitable for book designs that require glossy paper or many coloured inside pages, high resolution photographs, embossing or die-cutting, or hardcovers. Please refer to the technical specifications (page 47) to acquaint yourself with the possibilities and limitations of the print-on-demand approach.

Paper
Inside pages are printed most commonly on white 20# bond (roughly equivalent to 50# offset). Though the percentages vary from one mill run to the next, we seek to use paper with as much recycled content as possible. We also offer 60# offset paper (similar to 24# bond) and 20# certified 100% processed chlorine-free, alkaline, 80% post consumer recycled paper, both at an extra charge.

Covers are printed on card stock referred to in the printing trade as Coated 1 Side, 10 pt Carolina or similar.

Size
The inside pages are printed on 8.5 x 11 inches (about 216 by 279mm) paper and then cut down from that size. Common sizes are 8 [wide] x 10 [tall], 7 x 9, 6 x 9 and 5.5 x 8.5, though you may choose any dimensions you like. We cannot produce a cover flat large enough for perfect binding an 8.5 inch wide book of over 200 pages. Either this size must be coil bound or 3-hole punched, or you could opt for 8 inches wide to allow for a 1-inch spine thickness.

A fold-over front cover flap is ideal for coil-bound books

Bindings

You have a choice of plastic spiral coil, 3-hole punched or perfect bound. Descriptions of each can be found in the technical specifications. We have recently introduced a special fold-over front cover flap for coil-bound books so that the title can be printed on the flap and will be visible when the book is placed in a bookshelf with the binding inward ("reverse shelved").

Covers

Will buyers judge your book by its cover? You have a broad design choice here – including whether to hire an illustrator and graphic designer. All packages include two hours of a layout technician's time to prepare a colour cover suitable for one-at-a-time printing on a digital colour printer. This two hours is not considered "design" time – this is digital assembly of images and text following the author's instructions, and using supplied artwork and images. Expect up to 10% variance in each of the four components of the cover colours. This shifting is most noticeable with pastels and light colours – it is therefore advisable to design with rich, intense colours.

Trafford's role and responsibilities

Trafford staff will receive instructions, computer files, printout originals and possibly preprinted items from the author. These will be processed to become the digital master. A complete proof will be produced for the author's review. Master files will be kept ready to fill incoming orders promptly and accurately.

Author's role and responsibilities

The author is responsible for design and layout (typesetting) of the book, and submission as a PostScript (PRN format) file *or* as hardcopy printouts suitable for scanning. "Layout" includes you assigning fonts, sizes, margins, page numbering, etc., in a word processor or page layout program. If you need advice, assistance or a referral, please ask our staff.

Please clearly indicate your book's ISBN on all materials submitted. Once a proof is received, please review it carefully and notify us promptly of any concerns. If changes are required at this point, author's alterations (AAs) will be charged on a time-and-materials basis. Trafford will rectify its own errors without charge. As soon as the proof is 'signed off,' sales can begin!

Press clipping

"[Trafford] has something new to offer the world of publishing: a no-waste business system, where there are no warehouses full of unwanted books, because the book is printed only after the customer buys it."

—Simon Fraser University Peak

CHANGES AND UPDATES
Process, benefits and responsibilities

Benefit: you can make changes or updates at any time *(included in all three packages).*

Explanation
Each copy of your book is produced from a PostScript digital master that can be changed to reflect corrections or new information. This eliminates the need for including errata sheets or update notices.

Once your book is in its PostScript print format, there are no simple mechanisms for making changes such as "fix all the spelling mistakes" or "add a paragraph" or other text alterations – these generally must be made in the original word processor or page layout program and the resulting single pages or an entire new file is sent to Trafford. Trafford's technicians will then swap them page-for-page with the previous, offending pages.

Making these page substitutions is relatively straightforward. The author submits the replacement pages or files, following the same technical specs as during the original submission. Trafford's technicians revise the master file and print a complete proof for the author's review. The author is charged on a time-and-materials basis, with a minimum charge of one hour at US$48 (CDN$70) plus a new proof for US$15 (CDN$25).

Trafford's role and responsibilities
Trafford's technicians will replace pages or files on a time-and-materials basis. A bound proof will be sent for the author's confirmation. A new digital master file will be created and backed up.

Author's role and responsibilities
The author is responsible for preparing and submitting replacement pages, clearly explaining what is required and including a previous proof, if possible. Once a new proof is generated, the author confirms that it is satisfactory. Please include the ISBN with all materials and correspondence.

Measures of success

Doug Funk's research into his Icelandic heritage inspired him to write Rorkrüün: The Mystic Sword of Justerealm, *a tale about coming of age one millennium ago. Now retired, Doug credits his career as a salesman for honing his story-telling ability.*

COPYRIGHT AND AGREEMENT
Process, benefits and responsibilities

Benefit: you retain full copyright and may end the agreement at any time *(included in all three packages)*.

Explanation

Our close work with authors has consistently emphasized that authors view retaining their copyright as their highest single concern. Of course, anyone who has spent years writing a book understands the close emotional attachment (often a love/hate relationship!) that authors develop with their work.

By using Trafford's on-demand publishing service, the author does not surrender copyright, unlike in conventional author-publisher contracts. Instead, the author grants Trafford a nonexclusive license to publicize and sell copies of the book on the author's behalf, in exchange for royalties on sales. (With the Legacy package, Trafford does not handle sales for the author.) "Nonexclusive" means the author can sell copies personally or through other channels, including a contract with a trade publisher if one is offered. The author can end the agreement with Trafford at any point.

There are, of course, some writings with which Trafford will not be involved – we won't touch anything that appears to constitute hate literature, pornography, obvious libel or slander, or incites illegal activities, for example. Our author's contract stipulates that the author must guarantee clear copyright and no illegal content. If a book is too contentious to be on our shelves (in the eyes of readers), we reserve the right to end the contract at any point, refunding a portion of fees paid if appropriate.

Trafford's role and responsibilities

Trafford receives a nonexclusive license to publicize and sell copies of the book on the author's behalf, in exchange for royalties on sales. Please see the contract (page 57) for other responsibilities.

Author's role and responsibilities

The author grants to Trafford this nonexclusive license. You must guarantee clear copyright to all contents. (An excellent explanation about permissions and "fair use" of other authors' material may be found at www.copylaw.com.) You will guarantee the contents are not slanderous, libelous, pornographic, do not constitute hate literature, and do not incite unlawful acts. You agree that Trafford will be indemnified for lawsuits which arise over publication of your book.

Press clipping

"[Authors] dictate the price, and thus have the potential to make more on each book than through standard publishing."
—The Daily Courier, *Kelowna, BC*

MOVIE RIGHTS AND OTHER SALES
Process, benefits and responsibilities

Benefit: you retain all "other sales" or "subsidiary" rights *(included in all three packages).*

Measures of success

Columnist and entrepreneur Frederica Cere Kussin wrote AllEtiquette.com *as a guide to educate individuals on image, manners, business etiquette and international protocol for all continents.*

Explanation

The standard arrangement within the publishing industry stipulates that the book publisher will get half the revenues if a Hollywood producer comes knocking with a movie rights contract, or an overseas company wants to translate and sell the book in foreign markets. In fairness to trade publishers, they generally deserve to be well compensated for successfully chasing down those movie or foreign rights sales – since most of their best efforts don't yield results. With Trafford's on-demand publishing service, by contrast, the author has the copyright and receives all of any such extra revenues: for translations, foreign sales, movie rights and serialization, and for sales conducted personally or through trade publishers, wholesalers or distributors. The author is free to do as much (and as little) as desired to generate other sales, including engaging the services of agents and publicists.

Trafford's role and responsibilities

Trafford does not actively solicit other sales opportunities. Any offers or inquiries that we receive will be promptly forwarded to the author. You may find a suitable publicist or agent through our talent pool bulletin board at www.trafford.com/4dcgi/Talent.html.

Author's role and responsibilities

The author is free to do as much (or as little) as he or she wants to generate other sales, including engaging the services of agents and publicists. The author may also order copies at special 'author order' pricing and distribute them through whatever means are at his or her disposal.

PRICE AND ROYALTY
Process, benefits and responsibilities

Benefit: you set the retail price which determines the royalty amount (included in the Entrepreneur and Best Seller packages).

Explanation

The author decides the retail price and, in so doing, establishes the royalty amount. First, Trafford calculates the *single-copy printing cost* for the book based on production factors (number of pages, type of paper, type of covers, binding, etc.). See pages 62 and 63 for a chart of print costs. Next, the author decides the retail price based on his or her appraisal of the target audience. The retail price must be **at least 2.5 times the single-copy printing cost** to allow for a reasonable margin (to cover our costs and your royalties).

Various trade discounts are allowed to libraries and college bookstores (15%), Trafford's web bookstore (25%), other bookstores (40%) and distributors (48% or more). From the **net sale amount** (the retail price less the discount given) deduct the single-copy printing cost to determine the "**gross margin.**" The author's **royalty is 60% of the gross margin**. Your author services rep will calculate various price-point scenarios if you wish.

Please note that books published under the Entrepreneur package will not be sold at a trade discount to bookstores (other than the Trafford bookstore) or libraries or distributors – authors must upgrade to the Best Seller package to have this benefit.

When payments are received by Trafford from reselling situations such as sales of e-book digital downloads, the author will still receive 60% of the gross margin, the main difference being that the e-book retailer will have already determined and deducted the printing cost (downloading cost) from the net sales before sending Trafford the payment.

Trafford's role and responsibilities

Trafford calculates the single-copy printing cost, and publicizes the retail price set by the author. Trafford records royalties accruing to the author on each sale.

Author's role and responsibilities

The author sets the retail price and, in so doing, establishes the royalty.

Husband and wife authors David and Jennifer Ladewig have recently published Come Travel With Me To The Other Side Of Sunset *(his travel book) and* Amerikan Sunset *(her futuristic novel).*

Press clipping

"[Trafford's method] is so environmentally sound yet still promotes the free exchange and worldwide dissemination of ideas."

—*from University of Victoria* Standard

ACCESSING BOOK PROFESSIONALS
Process, benefits and responsibilities

Benefit: professional book services may be accessed through Trafford's website *(included in all three packages)*.

Explanation
Within the on-demand publishing system, the author is in control of, and is responsible for, editing, design and layout. The author may also wish to have additional publicity work performed beyond the services provided by Trafford.

Many authors already have considerable experience and talent that they can apply to preparing and promoting their books. Others may wish to contract book professionals to assist with various functions. For example, you may wish to seek out editors, ghostwriters, proofreaders, illustrators, book designers, typesetters and publicists in your own community.

Trafford provides a talent pool bulletin board service at our website (www.trafford.com/4dcgi/talent.html), listing book industry professionals who are prepared to work with authors in a long-distance working relationship. Each professional provides references that authors should verify to their own satisfaction – Trafford does not supervise nor guarantee any services provided by these independent professionals. Trafford's sole responsibility is offering to serve as the binding arbitrator in case of any disputes between an author and service provider. These professionals do not pay a fee to be included, but have all agreed to pay Trafford a 10% referral fee on work generated through this bulletin board. If clients are unhappy with a service located through our bulletin board, Trafford reserves the unilateral right to remove that professional's listing.

Trafford's role and responsibilities
Trafford maintains a bulletin board listing book industry professionals who are prepared to work with authors in other towns.

Author's role and responsibilities
The author may choose to hire book industry professionals locally or through Trafford's bulletin board. In either case, it remains the author's sole responsibility to contract for, approve and pay for all such work.

Measures of success

Marjory Harris was eighty-nine and legally blind when she first thought of writing. In Memories of the Moorish World and Beyond, *she describes in vivid detail her travels in abroad during the 1960s. She received great response and has now published two sequels,* Memories of South Pacific Islands *and* An African Safari *and* Memories of A Detour to Turkey.

SELLING AN E-BOOK VERSION
Process, benefits and responsibilities

Benefit: your book could be available for sale as a downloaded e-book (included in the Best Seller package only).

Explanation
A new vision of book publishing is being tested in the industry: e-books! It is an understatement to say the book industry is in a state of revolution. Some commentators believe there will be more changes to the industry over the next five years than have happened in the past two hundred years.

In November 2001, we began offering some titles as e-books, selling in downloadable PDF format. Authors need to be aware that no one can guarantee security from on-line piracy of your book. We will only arrange to sell for those authors keen on pioneering this new technology.

Trafford's role and responsibilities
Trafford will obtain the author's permission before licensing sales of a digital download version of any title. When revenues from sales are received by Trafford, 60% of that amount will be credited to the author's royalty account for payment on a quarterly basis. Trafford reserves the right to end the sale of the e-book version if revenues are below a level that covers maintenance costs.

Author's role and responsibilities
The author will decide to allow sales in an e-book version, or not. If agreeing, the author will set a retail price in consultation with Trafford staff.

Trafford's top-selling e-book is 100% Internet Credit Card Fraud Protected, *a short guide written by Vesper, a Russian writer who interviewed international credit card fraudsters. It was written to help Internet e-commerce companies avoid losses.*

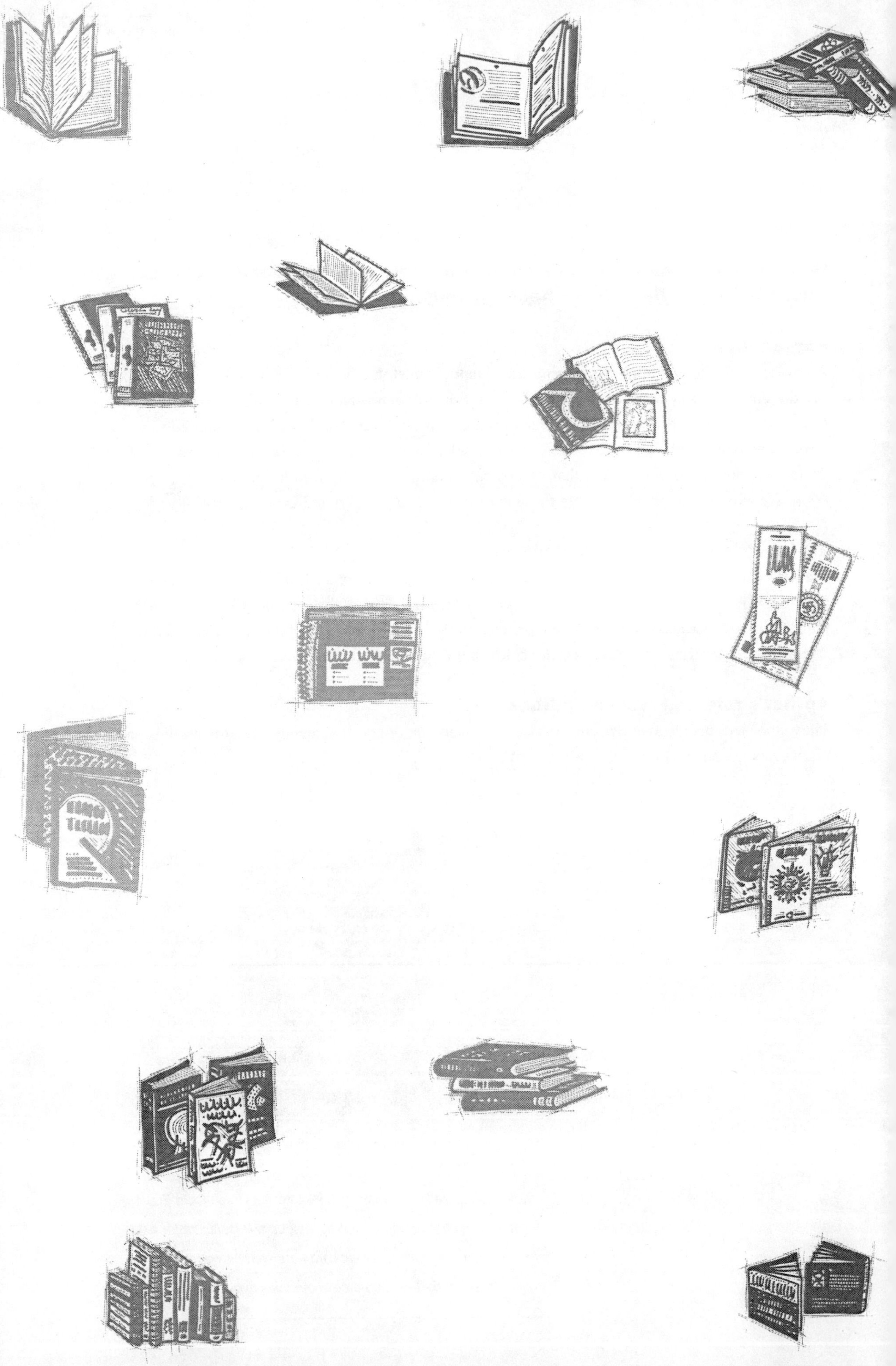

QUESTIONS AND ANSWERS

Sample questions from interested authors
Answers by publisher Bruce Batchelor

My manuscript is in Microsoft Word, how shall I send it? How many pages will it be if it is currently 78,000 words long and double-spaced?

Thanks for the question! Sounds like you have written a book, and are now at the stage where the manuscript needs to be "designed and typeset" before becoming a "real book." Trafford's publishing service essentially starts after your book has been designed and the "cover layout" and "page layout" (typesetting) have been performed. You can attempt doing the page layout yourself, or hire a graphic designer, or use Trafford's in-house layout service.

If you are thinking about doing the layout yourself, I can offer some advice… It is not too difficult, if you are fairly computer-savvy, to lay out your book using a word-processing program such as Microsoft Word or Corel WordPerfect. Although a dedicated design program (such as PageMaker and QuarkXPress) has more sophisticated features, nonetheless, many of our authors do create page layouts that are perfectly suitable for their needs using Word or Works or WordPerfect.

One tricky aspect is that word-processing programs will spontaneously repaginate the entire document to change what appears on each page. A 273-page book suddenly changes to become a 268-page or 275-page book! This "re-flow" obviously plays havoc with a table of contents or indices and other page-specific references. As well, when a Word file is printed on a different printer, or even moved to another PC, the resulting printout will likely be different from the original printout at your home or office. Yikes! The best "workaround" is for you to set up a "virtual printer" on your computer, let Word reflow the pages, then check on screen (view in *Print Preview*) and revise as needed. Then you create a PostScript print file (PS or PRN format) which will have the pagination *locked in*, and send that PostScript file to us via email, diskette or FTP upload. We have instructions for creating a PRN file that you can read on our website, or we can mail or fax them to you. **This might sound terribly complex, but our technical staff are available to coach you through the process over the phone – authors in their 90s have done this, so you "younger people" can do it, too!**

A graphic designer's fees to design and lay out a book can run from hundreds to thousands of dollars. We generally advise an author to expect about 10 to 15 hours of work, paying about US$48 per hour (CDN$70), for a novel or memoir. How-to books with illustrations, tables, pull-outs and the like can run to three or four times that amount. Trafford's staff can perform layout for a limited number of books on a fee-for-service basis. Please ask us to quote on your particular needs.

You also have the option to simply send us a crisp printout from the word processing program you have used and we'll scan each page as if it were a piece of artwork. The disadvantage of this approach is that the type in the final printed book will not be as crisp, and you won't have the option to sell your book as an e-book.

The author is responsible for ensuring a satisfactory design and layout of the book – satisfactory to the author and, of course, also effective for enticing people to purchase a copy. If a specific visual appearance is critical to your vision of the book and marketing strategy, and if you aren't experienced with book design, some consulting time with an experienced graphic designer could be in order. You might find someone in your local community – ask for a referral at a local print shop, or look on Trafford's talent bulletin board. A competent graphic designer should be able to create a print-ready digital original that looks crisp and handsome – ready for submitting to us for printing in-house, and for sale as an e-book (digital download).

The answer to your second question is: calculate for 300 to 420 words per page. Your 78,000 word manuscript, typeset in 6 x 9 final size, might be between 200 and 260 pages, depending on the choice and size of font, and amount of "white space" you prefer.

What formats and fonts should I use?

A professional graphic designer would say, "It depends on the design."

A do-it-yourselfer's trick is to find an existing book you admire and be "inspired" by the layout. Choose similar fonts and margins, then print out a sample of your work to compare side-by-side with that book's pages. **Please do NOT use Arial or Times New Roman** or any MultipleMasters as these fonts can cause "bugs" to appear when we print from the PostScript file.

Does Trafford edit the book? Does the fee include creating a cover illustration?

With our on-demand publishing service, the author is responsible for editing the contents and ensuring a satisfactory design or layout of the book and cover. If you wish to enlist help from an editor, proofreader, graphic designer, illustrator or other professional, you may be able to locate people in your local community (ask for a referral at a local print shop or talk to other writers), or look on Trafford's talent pool bulletin board at www.trafford.com/4dcgi/Talent.html.

All three publishing packages do include two hours of layout time to create a printable cover file. We'll work from your sketch, mock-up or digital file, and scan your artwork. Since a book really is judged by its cover, you may wish to consider a modest investment for a professional illustrator's handywork – this can make a huge difference to the final marketability of your book.

What will my publishing budget entail?

Your publishing budget will vary depending on the vision you have for your book. The outline below will give you an idea of the elements that you may wish to take into consideration. Keep in mind that not all of the following factors will apply to your book in particular. This budget is meant to give you a broad overview of the many options available to you as a self-publishing author.

>**Writing/Research: $_____**
>
>This expense depends on the stage that your book is at in the writing process. If the book is complete (aside from editing and proofreading), then this expense has already been accounted for (usually in terms of the hours of labour you have put in). If, however, the skills of a ghostwriter or researcher are still required, then the cost of these services will have to be factored into the publishing budget.
>
>**Editing/Proofreading**:
>> Substantive Edit: $ _____
>> Line Edit: $_____
>> Proofreading: $_____
>
>Once again, the stage that you feel your book is at will determine these costs. The book may require a substantive edit (i.e. a major overhaul – character and structure changes, etc.), it may only need alterations in grammar and sentence structure in the form of a line edit, or it may simply require a proofread.
>
>**Book Design/Typesetting: $_____**
>
>This expense depends on the design vision you have for your book. If a specific visual appearance is critical to your vision, and you aren't experienced with book production, some consulting time with an experienced graphic designer may be in order. You might find some-

one in your community, or look on Trafford's talent pool bulletin board on our website. Trafford's staff can also take on a limited number of layout assignments.

Illustrations: $_____

If you want illustrations inside your book and need someone to create them, factor in the cost. Your illustrator will want to know that our covers are produced on our digital colour copier 'on-demand' with quite good clarity and consistency. For the inside pages, black and white artwork (called "line art") and photos such as those you see in this Authors Guide are printed on-demand in toner.

Cover Artwork and Design: $_____

Once again, this can be elaborate (you may wish to hire an artist or graphic designer for special cover art and design) or very basic, and the cost varies accordingly. Keep in mind that a bold, simple cover can be as pleasing to the eye as a cover with a lavish design. You may wish to visit Trafford's talent pool bulletin board for professional assistance.

Trafford's Service: $_____ from $499 to $990 US ($699 to $1490 CDN)

Trafford's On-Demand Publishing Service™ has three packages that handle some or all of: publishing's legal and administrative tasks; some promotion and publicity; establishing sales channels across the Internet and at bookstores' special order desks; and fulfilling orders employing on-demand manufacturing. The chart on page 9 may help you match the package to your situation and aspirations.

Amendments, Updates and a Short Run of Books: $_____

Many authors elect to make a few minor changes once they see the final printed proof. Most authors buy a short run of books for distribution to friends and family, and for further promotional purposes. Once you've approved a proof, you may order in any quantity required. A printing cost list near the back of this guide will help you estimate costs for a short run.

Publicity and Advertising: $_____

This cost is really up to you, depending on how much of your own marketing you decide to do. There are many informative books on the subject that can be of help to you.

At the other side of the budget, you have **Potential Revenues**. These will come in the form of royalties, which are 60% of the gross margin on each sale. The retail price will be decided upon by you. We will be able to confirm the single-copy printing cost of your book (page 62 and 63) once we know all the tech specs. You can read more about royalties on page 35.

How are retail price and royalties established?

The author decides the retail price and, in so doing, establishes the royalty amount. Your royalty is 60% of the gross margin. Gross margin is net sale amount (retail price less trade discount) less print cost. Please see the information on page 35. Your Author Services Representative will help show you the royalties for various price scenarios.

Do I keep my copyright? How do I prove my copyright? What if a trade publisher offers me a contract? What if someone wants to buy movie rights?

You keep the copyright. Our work with other self-publishing authors has consistently emphasized that authors view retaining their copyright as their top single concern. Please see information provided on pages 15, 33 and 34. Your author services rep will help show you the royalties for various retail price scenarios.

Do you accept "anything" – or is there some quality control or censorship?

Some people (ironically this is seldom suggested by authors) imagine that an elite group of people should assess all books for 'literary worth,' perhaps mimicking the submission review process at trade publishers. An obvious problem with this viewpoint is that the publishing world's foremost experts in screening new book submissions repeatedly rejected writers and poets of the calibre of Virginia Woolf, Robbie Burns, Samuel "Mark Twain" Clemens, Zane Grey, Rudyard Kipling, Edgar Allen Poe, Robert W. Service, Henry David Thoreau and Margaret Atwood. Each of these literary giants (we could list hundreds of other equally illustrious and oft-rejected authors) had to self-publish to reach the public! Many nonfiction works rejected by publishers as 'not marketable,' such as the *Best of Bridge* cookbook series, were subsequently self-published and have sold millions of copies. Some books that were originally self-published, such as *The Joy of Stress, The Celestine Prophesy* and *The Christmas Box*, were subsequently picked up by major publishing houses who promoted sales to spectacular levels.

When an author devotes years of work to writing a book, we believe that person has a right to make it available to the public, within the limits of the law. There are, of course, some writings with which Trafford will not be involved – we won't touch anything that appears to constitute hate literature, pornography, obvious libel or slander, for example. Our author's contract stipulates the author must guarantee clear copyright and no illegal content. If a book is too contentious to be on our shelves (in the eyes of readers), we reserve the right to end the contract at any point, refunding a portion of fees paid if appropriate.

As a service to potential book buyers, we insist that every author provide at least an introduction or sample chapter for readers to peruse at Trafford's on-line bookstore. We don't edit a single word – readers get an accurate example of the content. We also show an image of the front cover, which may provide some indication of the visual appearance. That said, however, it should be noted that almost every author is fiercely proud of his or her book, and inevitably goes to great pains (and often considerable investment) to ensure top content and pleasing appearance. After all, the author's own name is on the book, and few of us write more than one book in our lifetime. Who wants to leave a shoddy piece of work as their literary legacy?

Can I use my own publishing company name?

Yes, some authors already do. Often this is set out as "published by SoAndSo Publishing in cooperation with Trafford Publishing" or "co-published by SoAndSo Publishing and Trafford Publishing – sales enquiries should be directed to Trafford" or a similar message.

An interesting phenomenon has begun with some early adopters of on-demand publishing – the creation of new 'virtual' publishing companies. A prime example of a new virtual company is Menagerie Press, which is really one person (Jan Lister Caldwell) performing the basic functions of a publishing house, such as finding promising works, editing, designing, publicizing, and ensuring that production and retail sales are happening. Menagerie just happens to use Trafford for production, retailing and some publicity. Menagerie launched *Cousin Clash* and its sequels by Jan and *My Secret Corner* and its sequel by Ruby Hunter Greenlaw. Jan plans to produce a few new books each year, selecting from her own writings and those of promising associates. Forming a new publishing company has never been simpler, and never required so little investment!

I expect we'll see virtual publishing companies popping up to sponsor many genres: specific forms of poetry, academic comment on a particular topic, conspiracy theorists, hobby how-to series, regional writers, and who knows what else.

Some people see on-demand publishing as a paradigm breakthrough in terms of democratizing book publishing. If it proves to be that significant, it's anyone's guess about all the ramifications.

Can I promote my book at my own website?
Yes, please do! We'll provide you with the HTML code to create a hyperlink from your website to your book's web page at Trafford's on-line bookstore where the actual financial transaction can occur.

We also encourage you to arrange publicity and hyperlinks at as many other websites as possible. A goal can be to ensure that everyone with an interest in your book's particular subject area (repairing guitars, calculus, rock groups, etc.) can readily learn about the book. Ask webmasters to post a link, introduce yourself as an author to chat room participants, join in discussions on newsgroup lists, and pass around an email version of your news release. People can't buy something they don't know about – so spread the word! Please note: you must not send unsolicited commercial emails – this is called *spamming* and can result in Trafford's server being shut down by Internet vigilantes.

What if I want a full-colour cover?
Good news – a full-colour cover and perfect binding are now included in all three packages. Covers are manufactured one-at-a-time while the inside pages are being printed. Lamination is available at a small extra cost. This 'manufacturing' happens on a digital colour laser printer and the results are somewhat more variable than with conventional printing. Authors requiring **exact** colour matching and consistency could have their covers offset printed in advance. We recommend that, if possible, you do not pre-print covers because this defeats one great advantage of on-demand publishing, which is *saving money by NOT preprinting*. Another consideration is that your pre-printed covers won't be on hand at our European printing plant, so your book won't be produced there.

What if I want my book to be a paperback?
No problem. Most authors want this appearance for their books. This 'perfect binding' is included in all three publishing service packages. We can also produce a spiral coil binding (with or without a fold-over flap for the title on a 'false spine'). A photo of the fold-over flap is on page 31.

How do I revise the contents after I get feedback from readers?
With on-demand publishing, it is simple to make revisions to produce a new edition. At any point, the author can send us replacement pages, either as digital files or hardcopy printouts, and we can swap them for the obsolete pages. Then we send the author a proof copy to ensure that everything is as planned. Trafford will bill you for technicians' time and materials, plus shipping of the proof.

If I do sign a deal with a trade publisher and stop using Trafford's service, does the book keep its ISBN?
Hey, we wish you good fortune with your New York publisher. And I'm also serious when I ask that if you get really famous, do you mind us telling others that you got your start here? Many authors – although by no means all – entertain thoughts about hitting the big time. If our collaboration can be a stepping stone to other ambitions, we're honoured to provide that service.

The ISBN actually isn't transferrable since a portion of the digits identify the publisher as Trafford. Your new publishing house will have its own sequence to assign. The ISBN system uniquely identifies the publisher, rather than the author, since that information allows bookstores and librarians to track down where to make a purchase.

Who chooses reviewers to whom complimentary copies will be sent?
The author. As the subject matter expert, the author is in the best position to know the appropriate journals or other media outlets where reviews might logically occur. The Best Seller package includes ten copies of your book which you can send to reviewers.

You may wish to send (via email, post and fax) a news release and query letter to see who wants a copy. Then it is entirely appropriate for you to follow up personally after a week or two to encourage the reviewer to pick your book from the stack he or she might have received that month. Often your phone call will provide the reviewer with a specific answer and marvellous quote from the author.

Whenever a review appears, please fax us a copy (with your ISBN on the cover sheet note), so we can add any glowing comments to your book's web page.

Where is my book's web page located? I have experience designing web pages, so can I design my own page?

The web page is located on Trafford's web server – we'll tell you the page's unique address so you can pass the URL to others and set hyperlinks to it. The web pages are actually generated (and updated nightly) by our proprietary ODP™ software from database fields, so there is no provision for authors to design their own pages.

If you have web designing talent, we urge you to create web pages promoting your book at other locations, and then refer potential buyers to the book's Trafford URL to complete the sale.

How are sales handled from customers in so many countries all using different currencies?

We now sell in two currencies (US and Canadian dollars). We plan to steadily add other currencies to make buying as convenient as possible for international customers: Euro and British pounds will be next. The author sets a retail price in each currency – the prices needn't be an exact correspondence. This allows for strategic pricing ending in .99 in each currency, if you wish. We calculate discounts, net sales, printing costs, then royalty amount accrued in the currency used by each buyer – and then convert that royalty credit into the author's preferred currency for payment.

I want to order 2,000 or 5,000 copies to place with a book wholesale company. Are there further discounts or savings for me as the author?

Yes! When the author orders such large quantities, the price per book drops dramatically. We'll tell you these figures once all the physical factors are finalized (such as number of pages, size, binding, type of cover, paper stock, inserts, etc.). You can check on pages 62 and 63 for prices. On larger print runs (over 5,000 copies), the price per unit decreases dramatically because offset presses, rather than digital copiers, are used. Ask for a quotation on specific quantities. A great advantage of on-demand publishing is that you can test market your book with short print runs before committing to an expensive large run.

I wish to have my books on the shelves of every bookstore across the country. Does Trafford make this happen?

I wish we could! A bit of math will illustrate the economics. Having five copies in every one of 20,000+ bookstores entails printing 100,000 copies at, perhaps, $3.00 each. Do you have $300,000? Plus another $500,000+ for shipping and advertising/promotions? Now consider that distributors and bookstores largely operate on a "returnable" basis, so you wouldn't see ANY income for about a year, and then you might get all 100,000 copies back instead!

Trafford does not extend such returnable/consignment terms to anyone – so such arrangements with resellers, if they happen, are side deals between the author (who buys a short run of books, pays for those, and takes the risk of them being returned) and distributor or bookstore, at whatever terms you negotiate. Some bookstores (including all the major on-line stores) will buy directly from Trafford on a non-returnable basis, but most authors generally buy 100 or 200 books and approach local and specialty bookstores themselves – with the bookstore paying 60% of retail price and the returnable/non-returnable terms being negotiated.

There isn't a smooth continuum between on-demand publishing with its non-returnable terms, and the book industry's standard mass distribution on a returnable basis. We have found no magic solution to bridge this gap. Self-publishing – even with help from a service such as Trafford's – entails the author learning a bit about the book industry… and you'll find it is a somewhat confusing, illogical business. However, once you've tested and proven a market demand, a major publisher may decide to gamble a few hundred thousand dollars to see your book on all those shelves.

Is there a maximum number of photos you can reproduce? In what form do I send them to you? I have 20+ photos. Most are black and white prints, but a few are colour prints, some are transparencies, and some were sent to me on email.

There is no limit to the number of photos you may include. However, I wish you to be aware of a number of considerations:

- the work (and cost) of preparing your manuscript for printing – typesetting, scanning photos, layout – is the author's responsibility in Trafford's system. You may be able to do this yourself, with a colleague, engage a local desktopper/graphic designer, or hire us to do the extra work. We can't work from slide transparencies, so you'll need to have prints made at a local camera shop.
- any image – no matter whether the original was a black & white print, colour print, transparency, or digital (TIF, EPS or JPG) – will end up as a scanned image of tiny black "dots" on a page in a PostScript file. (A colour image on the book's cover will be tiny dots of black, yellow, magenta and cyan.)
- the quality/clarity of the printed images will depend on two things:
    1. the talents and equipment of the person doing the scanning and layout, and
    2. the output device (we use laser printers which do an okay job with photos – there can be some "banding" through darker areas). The photos in this Guide are typical amateur shots.

    You are welcome to send a few test photos to see what a printed sample will look like.
- because of this "less-than-perfect" clarity and possible banding of photos and other screened illustrations, on-demand publishing simply may not be suitable for those book projects that are very dependent on crisp images. For example, a book full of photos intended to show off how good the photographer is… on-demand publishing won't serve that purpose with the current generation of printing equipment.

Measures of success

Katrina Robinson's book Poverty to Potential *is a detailed guide that helps people reach their life goals. She is committed to providing motivational workshops and lectures that will give people the tools to excel beyond social and economic barriers.*

Does Trafford provide me with names of people who have bought my book?

No, this would be a breach of the customers' privacy for those shopping at www.trafford.com. As well, we have no way of knowing who bought from resellers such as Chapters.Indigo.ca and Amazon.com. We'll provide general sales information with the quarterly royalty statement, but nothing that could identify individual buyers.

Will Trafford sell digital downloads of my book?

We have just begun to offer this option for selected Best Seller package titles. A digital file of the book (in PDF format) can be purchased at various e-book stores (including Amazon's) and downloaded onto the customer's computer for reading or printing out – with some security restrictions. The author sets the retail price and receives 60% of the gross margin, which works out to be about 30% of the retail price.

How often are royalties paid? Can I find out about sales each month and how many people have read the excerpt?

Royalties are paid quarterly about five weeks after the end of the quarter. We have a mechanism that allows authors to look up (on a confidential web page) their books' ongoing sales results and the amount of royalties accruing. Currently, we do not report on simple "hits" of how many potential customers have only browsed by without purchasing.

I envision my book as being large, full of colour photographs on glossy paper, and with a hardcover – is this possible using print-on-demand?

Print-on-demand produced books can be attractive and durable. There are, however, limitations to current manufacturing technology, and the type of book you describe is definitely outside those limitations. Such a book would have to be produced using offset printing, and probably would be economically published only through one of the larger publishing houses wanting to underwrite a lengthy press run (10,000 copies minimum).

Do you publish children's books?

Yes! We've published dozens of children's books. Our two all-time best sellers are *Cupid's Secret* and *When I Grow Up I Want to Be a Millionaire (A Children's Guide to Mutual Funds)* – both have delightful black & white illustrations. For a perfect-bound book the minimum number of pages is 50. In early 2003, we introduced an amazing breakthrough in on-demand full colour children's picture books. Please ask us for the guide called *Have You Written a Kids' Book?*

Why the name Trafford?

One of our founders, Steve Fisher, is an irrepressible Manchester United fan. Manchester United's home field is Old Trafford Stadium. Steve suggested the name because it stirs up fond memories for him.

Others have suggested that Trafford sounds like a neat blending of the words 'traffic' and 'afford,' which suggests Trafford Publishing will provide self-publishing authors with an affordable service and their books with some high-traffic exposure. It is our company's sincere aim to create successful experiences so the name Trafford will invoke great memories for everyone.

—Bruce Batchelor, publisher

TECHNICAL SPECS
What to know when designing and submitting your book

The print-on-demand concept
At the heart of print-on-demand technology is the concept of storing complete images of every page in a computer's memory. In technical terms, the images are stored as vector graphics or 600 dots per inch (dpi) bitmaps in PostScript format. When an order arrives, the appropriate paper stock is fed into a high-speed, duplexing laser printer. Then the digital file is recalled from memory and printed. The resulting pages (the "book block") are combined with a colour cover produced on a digital colour laser printer, and bound (generally spiral coil or perfect bound). Authors can choose to laminate the covers for books produced in our in-house print shop for an extra charge. The finished book is packaged and shipped to the bookbuyer, generally within 3 to 5 business days of the order being placed. While this is happening, credit cards are being verified, costs tabulated and royalties accrued in the author's account.

Appearance
The author (and the author's designer, if one has been hired) will wish to be aware of the range and bounds of our manufacturing capabilities. Books are produced literally on-demand, one-at-a-time in response to individual incoming orders. This is possible through use of high-speed, "print-on-demand" laser printers, and other printing and bindery machinery. Our duplexing laser copiers print full images of every page (of your book and everyone else's) from computer memory, at 600 dpi (dots per inch). There are limitations, of course, to what can currently be done one-at-a-time (printing and binding) on an economical basis. As the technology evolves, we are continually exploring ways to expand our manufacturing capabilities. We are already at the stage, however, where on-demand books can be attractive, practical and durable.

To date, most books marketed through Trafford have been information-intensive (training materials, novels, how-to guides, poetry, etc.), rather than image-intensive (such as coffeetable art books). Most books are produced in black and white (black toner on white paper) at a finished size of 8.5 [wide] by 11 inches [tall] or smaller – any dimension smaller is okay, such as 7 x 10, 6 x 9 or 5.5 x 8.5, for example, down to a minimum size of 5 x 5. An 8.5 x 11 book is actually about 8.25 by 10.75 since we do need to trim on three sides after perfect binding. 8.5 x 11 paper is about 216 by 279mm, slightly smaller than A4. In appearance, most Trafford titles are interchangeable with other softcover

Trafford's technology wizard, Gord Hooker, claims to be "just your average biker-nerd." His early deployment of Mac OSX technology for our servers and networks was featured on the www.apple.com website.

books and manuals found on your local bookstore shelves. Colour is generally reserved for the covers. Photos and other graphics are reproduced at a 106-line halftone screen, which is about a newspaper's image clarity.

Paper

We stock two weights (thicknesses) of white paper for the inside pages. These paper stocks are called 20# bond or 60# text weight paper (20# bond is approximately equivalent to 50# text weight; 60# text corresponds to 24# bond). As the weight increases, so does the opacity (text from the reverse side shows through less), and so do the cost, total book thickness and shipping weight. Most authors find 20# bond paper appropriate for their purpose. Both these stocks have some recycled content – typically 30% post-consumer.

We also offer 20#, certified 100% processed chlorine-free, alkaline, 80% post-consumer recycled paper, at the same price as the 60# text paper. See pages 62 and 63 for cost details.

Margins

Leave a minimum of .75 inches of white space on the inside of the page (where the book will be bound) and a minimum of .5 inches on the other three edges.

Size

At this point, books are manufactured on 8.5 x 11 stock, which means smaller books will be trimmed to size, and the extra paper discarded (recycled).

The most common sizes for books in North America are 8.5 inches wide x 11 inches tall (typically for workbooks, reports, technical manuals and training materials that are coil bound or 3-hole punched for a 3-ring binder); 8 x 10 or 7 x 9 (a mid-size for textbooks and other books with larger-format requirements); and 6 x 9 and 5.5 x 8.5 (for *paperbacks* and reference guides, and an increasing number of first-edition novels). Minimum size is 5 x 5 for perfect-bound, or 4 x 4 for spiral coil-bound. Maximum thickness is 700 pages.

Measures of success

Larry Welch is a storyteller at heart. His first book, Mary Virginia, A Father's Story, *was written as a gift for his daughter. He says, "Mary and I enjoyed her early years as the 'good old days' worth remembering in a little book."*

Bindings

Books can be bound in a number of fashions, with the choice made by the author to suit his or her vision of the published book. In the following explanations, *spine* refers to the edge of the book that is bound:

- **perfect bound:** this is the technical name for the binding on trade paperbacks... the pages are clamped together, then roughened along the face of the spine; hot glue is forced a tiny distance up between the pages, holding them to each other. Then a large cover sheet is glued and wrapped around the spine. The result is trimmed on three sides for an even appearance... advantages: this is the expected binding for novels and many other publications; title appears on the spine (important for bookstore and library shelves); inexpensive... disadvantages: book doesn't lie flat when opened; pages may come loose with rough use.
- **spiral plastic coil (black):** a row of small holes are punched about .25 inch (6mm) in from the spine and a coil is spiraled through to create a durable binding... Spiro is a common brand name... looks like an office report (which may or may not be appropriate for your book)... advantages: inexpensive, book opens flat (and folds back on itself), durable... disadvantages: title not visible on the spine; more expensive than perfect binding. *Note:* we can produce an extended flap on the front cover of a coil-bound book; this flap folds over the open side of the book and forms a 'false spine' where the title may be printed, so the book's title is visible when stored on a bookshelf.
- **3-hole punched (without 3-ring binder):** if your book is a reference manual that might be updated later, 3-hole paper may be the answer... the pages are shrink-wrapped for protection during transit... advantages: expected by users of technical manuals... disadvantages: binders are not stocked here, user is expected to have or acquire one.

> **Press clippings**
>
> *"Now, a new publishing age is dawning. By taking advantage of recently developed on-demand printing technologies, along with the blooming of the World Wide Web, publishers or authors can publish books that may appeal to a narrow market, even a small audience widely dispersed around the world."* — in 'Trafford Publishing does it all for you,' an article in Print On Demand Business Magazine

Submitting the inside pages

Whether it is the author or a graphic designer who will be preparing the inside pages (the "bookblock"), the submission guidelines are the same, and you have many choices:

- If the submission is a **previously-published book** and you are submitting a bound copy, it will be necessary for us to remove the binding before scanning. Please be aware that scanning produces a darker and less crisp result compared to the original. The final book will have the clarity of a photocopy of the original.
- If you are submitting a **typed manuscript for transcribing and then typesetting** (you will be paying extra fees for this work), please do not send us your only copy! Make a back-up copy to keep in a safe place. Include photocopied pages from a book you admire so we can emulate that book's design when laying out yours.
- If you are submitting a **Word** (or Works or WordPerfect) **file for layout/typesetting** (you will be paying extra fees for this work), please include a full printout plus photocopied pages from a book whose design you admire.
- If you are doing the book layout yourself – possibly in Microsoft Word – and will be submitting the pages as a **ready-to-print digital file** (PostScript PRN print format – *see next paragraph*), please also supply us with a complete paper printout so we can verify that the results at our end match those at your end. We require a PostScript file because otherwise even the smallest incom-

patibility of software versions, printer drivers, fonts and platforms can change page breaks and sabotage your careful design. We'll devote up to two hours of our technicians' best efforts to ensuring that your digital file's output matches the accompanying hardcopy printout. Occasionally we may have to scan from the hardcopy, or ask for a more compatible digital file, or charge for extra technician's time and materials – we'll advise you before running up charges, so you make the choice.

Best digital results are possible if you create a PostScript file (by using "print to file/disk" to make a PRN or PS file) using the appropriate print driver (look for "LaserWriter Select 360" which is standard on both Macintosh and Windows operating systems, or it can be downloaded from www.apple.com). For whatever reason, PostScript fonts generally work better than TrueType ones, so try to use PostScript fonts. **Please do NOT use Arial or Times New Roman** or MultipleMaster fonts. Our technical crew will be happy to coach you through this PRN-creating process. See also the instructions at www.trafford.com/4dcgi/prn.html.

- To submit the **ready-to-print original for scanning as a paper printout** (techies call this a "hardcopy original" or a "camera-ready mechanical"), use a 600 dpi or better printer with good-quality white bond paper. Single-sided originals are best, with notes attached to indicate placement of any intentionally blank pages. If the finished size is to be less than 8.5 x 11 inches (216 x 279mm), include cropmarks on the top sheet only. Do not cut your printouts down to the final size – leave them as 8.5 x 11 pages.
- If you are sending a document as a **PageMaker, Quark or InDesign file**, please enclose all fonts and images used within the document. Like any other print service, we can make no hard-and-fast guarantees that results at our end will exactly match your hardcopy printout – but we can promise to do our best. For optimal results (professional kerning and tracking, stable pagination, etc.), we strongly recommend using only PostScript fonts. Files from other programs such as Word or WordPerfect are welcome, though you **must** create a PRN or PS file as discussed above.
- Some authors pick a page size of 5.5 x 8.5. Do NOT turn your file into a booklet ("imposed") for printing two pages on one side of a sheet. We do not print two-up. Simply centre the page image on a basic 8.5 x 11 sheet.

Covers

Authors have a choice of covers, from simple to elaborate. Having a full-colour cover is included in all three on-demand book publishing packages. Lamination is optional at an additional cost (for coil-bound books of any thickness and perfect bound books of 100 pages or more). This technology is not ideal: although they are more durable, laminated covers may curl noticeably as humidity levels change.

If the binding is a coil, then there is a front and back cover. If the book is to be perfect bound, the front and back covers and spine are formed from a single large sheet (referred to as a "cover flat"). We cannot print on the inside of the cover.

Included in all three publishing packages is two hours of technician's time to lay out the cover – working from either a digital file from a designer, or from your own file and artwork to produce a digital, print-ready file. Authors wanting a specific cover look can prepare it themselves, or engage the services of a graphic designer and possibly an illustrator or photographer. Trafford can provide referrals if you wish.

Specifications for colour cover design

- Scan colour photos and art to be 200 to 300 dpi at final size. Anything above 300 dpi will be automatically reduced to 300 dpi. Submit cover images in Photoshop or TIF format, with CMYK setting (not RGB).

- Placement of type and barcodes or any vital part of the image must be 1/4 inch inside the crop marks. Plus there should be a full 1/8 inch bleed outside the trim line.
- We recommend you avoid placing any long vertical or horizontal lines (including sides of photos) within 1/2 inch of the edges – as these will accentuate any small discrepancies in trimming.
- Lettering on the spine is generally oriented so it can be read when the book is placed flat on the table, front cover up. Minimum spine thickness is 100 pages (50 sheets) if you wish the title to appear on the spine. You cannot have a colour break (change) at the spine of the perfectbound book of less than 100 pages.
- There will be variations (up to 10%) on any of the four colour components from day to day – this is an inherent limitation of using a colour laser printer – so you may wish to avoid pastels and light colours and design with bolder, richer colours with lots of contrast.
- The spine thickness may be measured according to the following ratios, depending on the weight of paper used for the inside pages. Maximum spine thickness for perfect binding is 700 pages of 20# bond (about 1.35 inches). Maximum for coil binding is 520 pages of 20# bond (one inch).

    Inside pages on 20# bond .... 520 pages (260 sheets) = 1 inch (25.4 mm)
    60# offset .... 450 pages (225 sheets) = 1 inch

The formula for spine thickness with 20# bond is (# of pages) * .002 inches
The formula for spine thickness with 60# offset is (# of pages) * .00225 inches

- Minimum number of pages for perfect binding is 100 pages (50 sheets) if the cover is laminated; 50 pages (25 sheets) if the cover is not laminated.
- We will supply your designer with the barcodes and Trafford colophon (logo) as electronic files (EPS format) – or you can indicate where we are to place the barcode and logos.

Notes about photos and screens on the inside (black and white) pages.

Inside pages (the "book block") are printed at 600 dpi. Our output devices have characteristics that a designer will wish to know.

- Scan photos at 200 dpi greyscale; scan black and white artwork at 600 dpi bitmap setting.
- When setting the levels on photographs, set your white point at 5% to avoid excessive specular highlights. Set your black point at 95%, depending on the photo.
- Avoid large areas of more than 95% black (such as a large black box with reversed type) as this may cause ghosting. This includes photos that have large, dark areas on them. For such photos, set your black point at 90%.
- Expect some streaks and banding – unavoidable with laser-printing technology. Lightening your photos will make this less noticeable. You are welcome to send trial prints to test the output.
- Set the line screen setting to 106 lines per inch.
- Any screen or tint of less than 5% may not be visible on the output; over 95% may appear black.

Here are example screens:

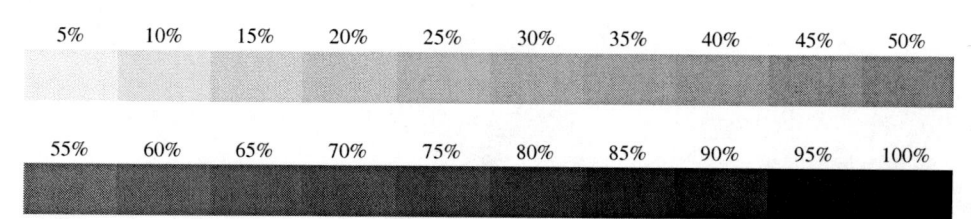

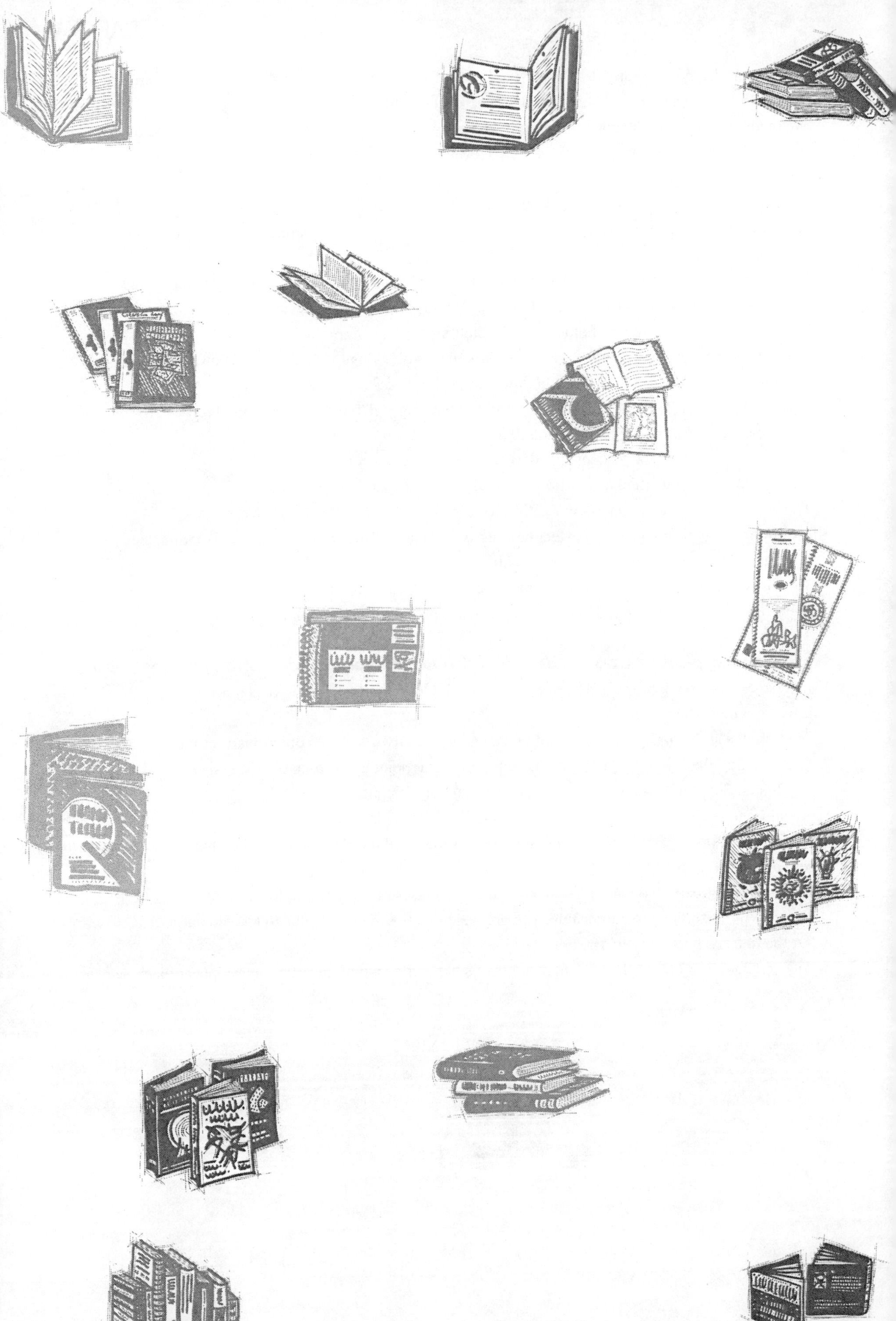

AUTHOR CHECKLIST
Devoting careful attention to tasks will ensure steady progress

During the publishing process, the author has many important responsibilities, most of which are listed on this sheet. Trafford author services staff have a corresponding (and much longer) list of their responsibilities. By progressing steadily through these checklists, you and Trafford's staff will be devoting the careful attention to this process that your book deserves!

	TASK	DESCRIPTION
❏	Complete & sign agreement	The agreement is in this Authors Guide or can be printed from our website. Fax the signed agreement with credit card number, expiry date and name on the card to 250-383-6804 (US East Coast authors, fax to 252-633-4816). Or mail or courier it to Trafford with a cheque or credit card information. If you don't already have your own copy of the Authors Guide, tell us and we'll send one right away.
❏	Complete & submit metadata form	The metadata form is in this Authors Guide or may be found at our website. It can be mailed, couriered, faxed or emailed. It is particularly helpful if the lengthier information (descriptions and sample excerpts) is submitted on disk or via email.

[we'll return a receipt, an ISBN to identify your book, and introduce your author services rep]

❏	Prepare & submit originals	Ensure design and layouts for covers and inside pages fall within technical specifications (see pages 49–51); send originals to Trafford (keep backups yourself); include paper printout when sending digital files; include clear instructions about binding, paper, size, cover and other aspects. Mark package "business documents only, no commercial value."

[we'll prepare a master digital print file, then send you a bound "proof"]

❏	Review & sign off the proof	Advise us the proof is satisfactory.

[we'll calculate cost to manufacture single copies "on-demand"]

❏	Set the retail price & royalty	Set your retail price at least 2.5 times the single copy printing price to ensure an adequate royalty. Retail price minus bookseller's discount = net sale amount; then subtract the single-copy printing cost to obtain the gross margin… your royalty is 60% of the gross margin.

[for Entrepreneur and Best Seller authors, we'll inform you when your book's web page is ready for you to proofread]

❏	Notify us that you've read & approved the web page	

[we'll activate your book's webpage and – if you selected the Best Seller package – submit information to key search engines, send out the announcement, submit info to key retailers and distributors, and mail you ten copies of your book, postcards and announcement cards…]

❏	Have a publishing launch party!	Go wild and celebrate! Authors are expected to be fairly eccentric, so you have considerable latitude in dress and behaviour.

METADATA FORM

Fill in this form so we can start on cataloguing and your web page!

About the author

Full legal name ....

Name of author as appearing on title page ....

Citizenship .... Date of birth (year/month/day) ....

Is it okay to show your birth year in CIP data to be printed inside book? ....

Additional names appearing on title page – please include full names, dates of birth, citizenship and function (e.g. co-author, editor, illustrator)

....

....

Mailing address

Organization (if applicable) ....

Street ....

City .... State/province ....

Country .... Zip/postal code ....

Courier address (if different from above) ....

Email address ....

Royalties cheques payable in which currency?   USA dollars   or   Canadian dollars   *(circle one)*

May we deposit your royalties directly into your credit card account?   Yes   No   *(circle one)*

   If yes, please provide details ....

Canadian authors only: if GST is due on royalties, provide GST number ....

How did you hear about Trafford? Did anyone provide information (such as a brochure or Internet hyperlink) to recommend our service? ....

Did you use the services of anyone from our talent pool? ....

About the book

(This info is used to create your book's web page, to inform e-retailers and search engines, and to submit to the librarian-cataloguers who create a Cataloguing-in-Publication Data listing. It is helpful if you email us the longer descriptions. Thanks!)

Full title of your book ....

Binding type? Perfect Bound or Spiral Coil *(circle one)*

Cover to be laminated? Yes   No *(circle one)* [Please note: this adds us$1.25 to the retail price and laminated covers may curl noticeably with changes in humidity. Available for books over 100 pages.]

Approximate number of pages ....   Desired final size (width by height) ....

Is there an alphabetic subject index at the back of the book?   Yes   No   *(circle one)*

Has this book been published before (including self-publishing)? Please describe, including date, ISBN, etc. ....

Is there a bibliography? .... Bibliographic references? ....

Is there an introduction?............. Is there a preface? .... Is there a Table of Contents? ....

Is this book the proceedings of a conference? (If yes, please provide details)......................................

Is this book part of a series? (If yes, please provide details, including name of series).......................

Type of book (e.g., novel, textbook, poetry, etc.) ....

Intended audience (e.g. general, professional, children)..

Primary subject of the book (e.g. self-help, automotive, fiction) ....

Keywords (up to 12) a potential customer might use when searching for your book at an Internet search engine ....

....

....

Full book description (one or two paragraphs – attach additional sheet if necessary, or email this to us). *This is used for the "About the Book" part of your book's webpage and will also be submitted to online booksellers* ....

....

....

....

....

....

Brief description or "teaser" for book (your "sales pitch" in 30 words or less). This teaser will be used for your book's announcement ....

....

....

....

....

Author's biographical note (attach additional sheet if necessary, or email this to us). *This is used for the "About the Author" part of your book's webpage*

....

....

....

....

....

Author's photo to be shown on website?   No   Yes   *(circle one)* If yes, please enclose a print or digital image. *If you want the photo also on your book's cover, please indicate that clearly on your cover mock-up and instructions.*

Identify or attach excerpts to be used as sampler on web page (e.g., introduction, chapter X, table of contents, etc.). Indicate priority if suggesting more than one – there is generally room for about 6 or 7 pages from your book ....

....

....

Additional comments

....

....

....

That's it, you've completed this task. Send this form to us and we can start the publishing process!

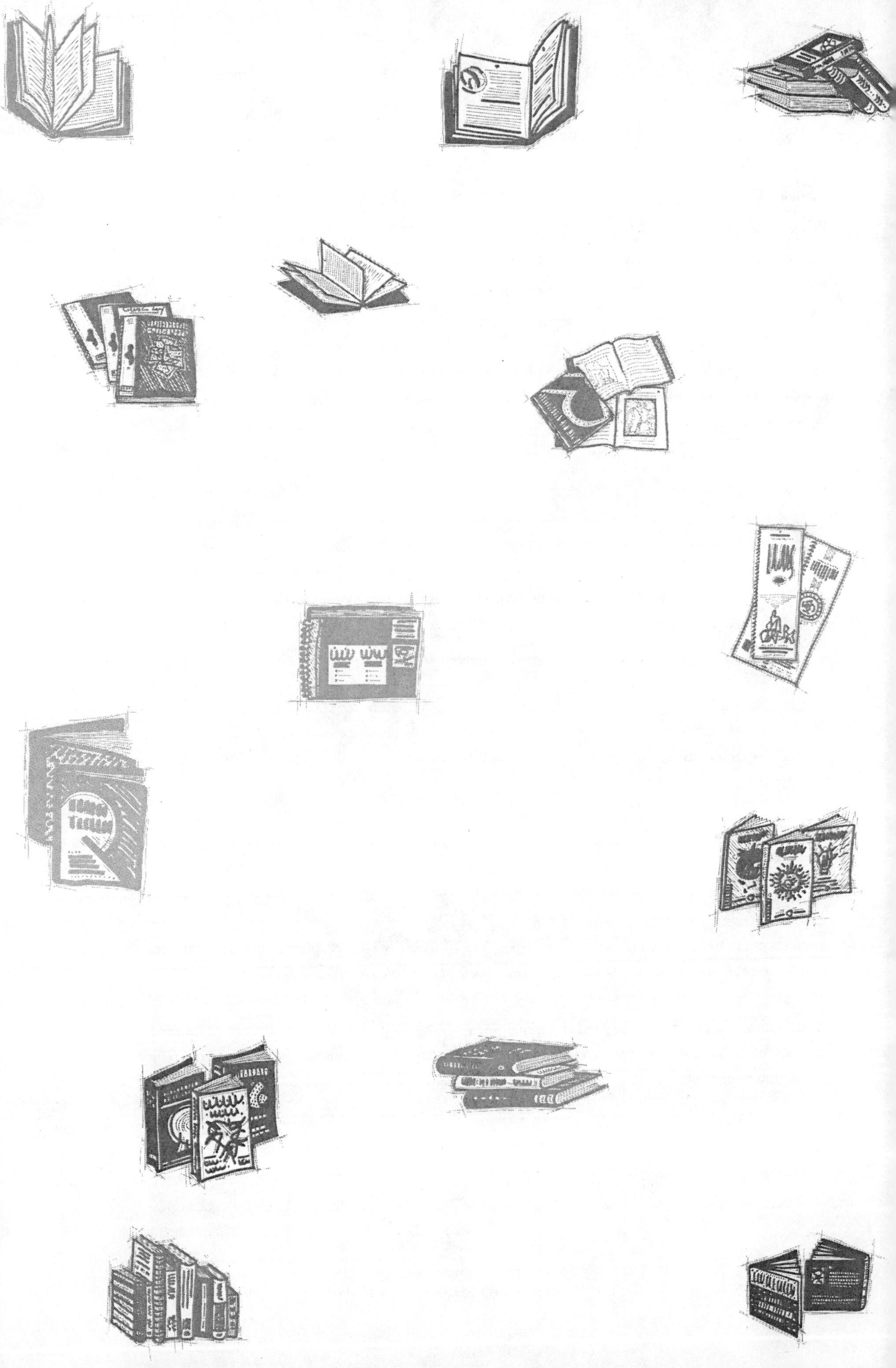

CONTRACT
Trafford on-demand publishing service™ agreement

TRAFFORD

THIS IS THE PUBLISHING AGREEMENT BETWEEN THE AUTHOR AND TRAFFORD PUBLISHING ON THIS _____ DAY OF _____, _____.

• enter date

BETWEEN:

(name of person or organization, called herein the **"Author"**):

• enter your name, the book's title, and your contact information

_____

(full mailing address) _____

_____

_____

(Social Security Identification (SSI) number for USA residents)

_____

(Employer Identification Number (EIN) for USA corporations & agencies)

_____

(phone) _____

(fax) _____

(email) _____

(title(s) of work(s)) _____

THE FIRST PARTY,

AND:

definitions

TRAFFORD PUBLISHING, A DIVISION OF TRAFFORD HOLDINGS LTD. Suite 6E, 2333 Government Street, Victoria, BC, Canada V8T 4P4 (called herein "**Trafford**"), **THE SECOND PARTY**.

Generally it is understood that the Author is the creator of the work and holder of the copyright, or has legal authority to publish the work.

The "**work**" (also referred to herein as the "**book**") is a book, manuscript, or work of art or other document provided by the Author, to which this agreement pertains.

Trafford provides the Trafford On-Demand Publishing Service™ to self-publishing authors. This service makes the work available for retail sales to the public by combining conventional publishing tasks, print-on-demand manufacturing and Internet web publicity and retailing. Specific features of this service vary according to the author's selection between publishing packages offered. This service may also include selling the book as an electronic file (e-book).

continued...

v 19e

Trafford offers to do the following for the author:

price schedule

*select a publishing package by circling 1, 2 or 3

1. Provide the "Best Seller" Trafford on-demand publishing service™ package for $990.00 (U.S.); or

2. Provide the "Entrepreneur" Trafford on-demand publishing service™ package for $679.00 (U.S.); or

3. Provide the "Legacy" Trafford on-demand publishing service™ package for $499.00 (U.S.);

4. Provide such other publishing services as may be required by the author at a mutually agreed price;

5. Provide to Canadian customers the services above at the following rates:
   Item 1, Best Seller Package: $1490.00 (Canadian)
   Item 2, Entrepreneur Package: $969.00 (Canadian)
   Item 3, Legacy Package: $699.00 (Canadian).
   Canadian residents will add 7% Goods and Services Tax (GST) to all above prices unless exempt.

description of our service begins

6. **Provide the Trafford on-demand publishing service™ package** which includes the following services:
   Items marked by **L** indicate those included in the Legacy package,
   Items marked by **E** indicate those included in the Entrepreneur package,
   Items marked by **B** indicate those included in the Best Seller package

7. **Legal and Administrative**
   (1.) arrange an International Standard Book Number (ISBN), Cataloguing-in-Publication Data entry and Bookland EAN and UPC barcodes unless otherwise directed by the Author, and typeset the frontmatter pages accordingly; **(L, E, B)**
   (2.) include a copyright notice intended to protect the author's rights in all copies of the book produced; **(L, E, B)**
   (3.) deposit two dated copies with the Canadian National Library; **(L, E, B)**
   (4.) provide accounting of sales and pay royalties on a quarterly basis; **(E, B)**
   (5.) provide ten (10) bound copies without charge for the author's use; **(B)**

8. **Publicity**
   (1.) with the author's input, create promotional and descriptive text for the Trafford bookstore catalogue found at www.trafford.com on the Internet **(E, B)**, for the announcement **(B)**, and for the book's web homepage (web page); **(E, B)**
   (2.) create and maintain the book's individual web page **(E, B)** and notify search engines and directories of its contents; **(B)**
   (3.) broadcast by email an announcement to a list of industry and media contacts; **(B)**
   (4.) provide the code for hyperlinking to the book's web page; **(E, B)**
   (5.) provide 250 publishing announcement cards; **(B)**
   (6.) provide 100 colour postcards showing the book's cover; **(B)**

continued...

9. **Sales Channels**
(1.) make the book available for retail purchase by individual customers at Trafford's bookstore (at www.trafford.com), through Internet web order form, email, phone, fax and mail, accepting credit cards and corporate and government purchase orders, with a discount provided to Trafford's bookstore as per Trafford's standard schedule; (**E, B**)
(2.) provide bookstores, libraries and distributors with discounts on Trafford's standard schedule; (**B**)
(3.) submit information on the book for sale through other on-line bookstores; (**B**)
(4.) sell copies at a discounted price to the Author for other distribution, as requested by the Author; (**L, E, B**)
(5.) submit the book for sales as an electronic file, where deemed feasible by Trafford; (**B**)

10. **Production and Order Services**
(1.) create an electronic image master of the book, either through scanning the paper version or printing from an electronic file or a combination of the two methods, at the discretion of Trafford, allowing 2 hours of technician's time, in a format suitable for prompt retrieval and on-demand printing; (**L, E, B**)
(2.) produce a complete bound proof and submit this for the Author's review and make, without charge to the Author, any corrections to the master which arise from errors by Trafford's staff or mechanical/electronic malfunction; (**L, E, B**)
(3.) determine a single-copy printing cost (**L, E, B**) and minimum retail price (**E, B**) to be used by the Author in establishing the retail price;
(4.) archive the master file for the duration of this agreement; (**L, E, B**)
(5.) manufacture books on demand as orders are received and fulfil orders promptly, with median times of less than 5 days if possible (allow longer for large print runs); (**L, E, B**)

11. **Make royalty payments on a quarterly basis** to the Author for each copy of the work sold, with the royalty being 60% of the gross margin (retail price less trade discount, less single-copy printing cost). (**E, B**)

The Author accepts the offer of Trafford and agrees to the following to create the contract:

partial list of what you, as the author, are responsible for

12. **The Author will perform several tasks**, including the following:
(1.) provide a usable electronic file of the book or scan-ready paper originals, and specifications for the book's appearance, including choice of binding, type of cover, paper stock, size and other factors; (**L, E, B**)
(2.) provide, or arrange and pay for the production of, any items required by the Author which are not appropriate for print-on-demand production; (**L, E, B**)
(3.) promptly review the bound proof; (**L, E, B**)
(4.) determine a reasonable retail price in consultation with Trafford; (**E, B**)
(5.) prepare, in cooperation with Trafford's staff, promotional text for use on Trafford's web bookstore and on the book's web page (**E, B**) and for the announcement; (**B**)

continued...

(6.) if the Author has his or her own Internet homepage(s), the Author will put a prominent hyperlink to the book's web page at Trafford's bookstore. (**E, B**)

13. **The Author further agrees**:

more obligations of the author

(1.) to provide the money as specified in Trafford's offer of services as set out above;
(2.) to provide assurance that the Author has and always will retain copyright to the work published by this agreement. It is understood the Author shall always have the right to publish their work elsewhere if they wish. The Author is agreeing to hire Trafford to produce and market the work and collect the royalties and distribute them according to this agreement, nothing more.
(3.) to allow Trafford to distribute promotional copies of the book free of charge and free of royalties to the Author as Trafford deems necessary, providing this is at no cost to the Author;
(4.) that Trafford's customer list is private and confidential and will always remain Trafford's property;
(5.) to accept the right of Trafford to refuse to publish any content in breach of Canadian laws at their sole discretion;
(6.) to eliminate any defamatory or unlawful content and to assume any and all liability for content and to hold Trafford harmless from any liability arising from content of the Author.

14. THE PARTIES BOTH UNDERSTAND:

mutual obligations, etc.

(1.) This agreement is non-exclusive. The author may enter into other publishing agreements concurrently with this agreement.

(2.) Either party may terminate this agreement at any time on delivering immediate written notice without any necessary cause provided only that all outstanding compensation becomes the respective party's debt and pre-existing payment obligations remain on both parties;

(3.) The laws of the Province of British Columbia, Canada, shall apply and the parties agree to use binding arbitration in British Columbia to resolve any irreconcilable dispute between the parties;

(4.) Trafford will not warrant the website at www.trafford.com being uninterrupted or error-free. Trafford agrees to use due diligence and reasonable care in maintaining its website;

(5.) Changes to this contract may be necessary from time to time to reflect evolution of Trafford's service to self-publishing authors and the author will be notified in such an eventuality, provided either party retains the right to terminate at any time without liability for any damages from this contract except payment of outstanding royalties and any other outstanding debts;

you always retain copyright

(6.) The Author at all times retains whatever copyright and other publishing rights they possessed at the time this agreement is signed.

(7.) Trafford may subcontract all or parts of its service to other divisions and subsidiaries fo Trafford Holdings Ltd.

continued...

This agreement is the full agreement and all its terms.

The parties, having read and agreed to the above, sign this document in witness of their agreement:

• you and a witness sign here, and send it to us for our signature (we'll send back a signed copy for your records)

_____	_____
The Author	Trafford Publishing
_____	_____
Witness	Witness

The Author has read and accepts all provisions of this Agreement, and the Author makes payment as follows:

Canadian residents: remember to include 7% GST

Amount: $ _____ . ____   in US funds   in Cdn. funds *(circle one)*

❑ Enclosed cheque

or

❑ CREDIT CARD number _____
cardholder's name _____
expiry date _____

❑ Visa   ❑ MasterCard   ❑ Amex

or

❑ Purchase Order (gov't and institutions only)
_____   dated _____

Please note: to expedite the start of our service for your book, please remember to fill in the Metadata Form (page 54) and send it to us with the signed contract.

Authors on the US East Coast who have been in contact with staff in our North Carolina office, please contact Carol Reed for the Trafford Publishing, Inc. version of this contract.
Email to coreed@trafford.com
Phone toll-free 1-888-240-3723   Fax 252-633-4816

v 19 e

TRAFFORD

Single-copy Book Printing Cost in USA $

Print cost = what you, as author, pay for copies of your own book   Retail price = what a bookstore's customer pays for your book

# of Pages	Single-copy print cost	50 + (-3%)	100 + (-6%)	250+ (-9%)	500+ (-12%)	1000+ (-15%)	Min. Retail Price
50	$ 3.33	$ 3.23	$ 3.13	$ 3.03	$ 2.93	$ 2.83	$ 8.33
100	$ 4.15	$ 4.02	$ 3.90	$ 3.77	$ 3.65	$ 3.52	$ 10.36
110	$ 4.31	$ 4.18	$ 4.05	$ 3.92	$ 3.79	$ 3.66	$ 10.77
120	$ 4.47	$ 4.34	$ 4.20	$ 4.07	$ 3.93	$ 3.80	$ 11.18
130	$ 4.63	$ 4.49	$ 4.35	$ 4.22	$ 4.08	$ 3.94	$ 11.58
140	$ 4.80	$ 4.65	$ 4.51	$ 4.36	$ 4.22	$ 4.08	$ 11.99
150	$ 4.96	$ 4.81	$ 4.66	$ 4.51	$ 4.36	$ 4.21	$ 12.39
160	$ 5.12	$ 4.97	$ 4.81	$ 4.66	$ 4.51	$ 4.35	$ 12.80
170	$ 5.28	$ 5.12	$ 4.97	$ 4.81	$ 4.65	$ 4.49	$ 13.21
180	$ 5.45	$ 5.28	$ 5.12	$ 4.95	$ 4.79	$ 4.63	$ 13.61
190	$ 5.61	$ 5.44	$ 5.27	$ 5.10	$ 4.93	$ 4.77	$ 14.02
200	$ 5.77	$ 5.60	$ 5.42	$ 5.25	$ 5.08	$ 4.90	$ 14.43
210	$ 5.93	$ 5.75	$ 5.58	$ 5.40	$ 5.22	$ 5.04	$ 14.83
220	$ 6.10	$ 5.91	$ 5.73	$ 5.55	$ 5.36	$ 5.18	$ 15.24
230	$ 6.26	$ 6.07	$ 5.88	$ 5.69	$ 5.51	$ 5.32	$ 15.64
240	$ 6.42	$ 6.23	$ 6.03	$ 5.84	$ 5.65	$ 5.46	$ 16.05
250	$ 6.58	$ 6.39	$ 6.19	$ 5.99	$ 5.79	$ 5.60	$ 16.46
260	$ 6.75	$ 6.54	$ 6.34	$ 6.14	$ 5.94	$ 5.73	$ 16.86
270	$ 6.91	$ 6.70	$ 6.49	$ 6.29	$ 6.08	$ 5.87	$ 17.27
280	$ 7.07	$ 6.86	$ 6.65	$ 6.43	$ 6.22	$ 6.01	$ 17.68
290	$ 7.23	$ 7.02	$ 6.80	$ 6.58	$ 6.36	$ 6.15	$ 18.08
300	$ 7.40	$ 7.17	$ 6.95	$ 6.73	$ 6.51	$ 6.29	$ 18.49
310	$ 7.56	$ 7.33	$ 7.10	$ 6.88	$ 6.65	$ 6.42	$ 18.89
320	$ 7.72	$ 7.49	$ 7.26	$ 7.03	$ 6.79	$ 6.56	$ 19.30
330	$ 7.88	$ 7.65	$ 7.41	$ 7.17	$ 6.94	$ 6.70	$ 19.71
340	$ 8.05	$ 7.80	$ 7.56	$ 7.32	$ 7.08	$ 6.84	$ 20.11
350	$ 8.21	$ 7.96	$ 7.72	$ 7.47	$ 7.22	$ 6.98	$ 20.52
360	$ 8.37	$ 8.12	$ 7.87	$ 7.62	$ 7.37	$ 7.11	$ 20.93
370	$ 8.53	$ 8.28	$ 8.02	$ 7.76	$ 7.51	$ 7.25	$ 21.33
380	$ 8.70	$ 8.43	$ 8.17	$ 7.91	$ 7.65	$ 7.39	$ 21.74
390	$ 8.86	$ 8.59	$ 8.33	$ 8.06	$ 7.79	$ 7.53	$ 22.14
400	$ 9.02	$ 8.75	$ 8.48	$ 8.21	$ 7.94	$ 7.67	$ 22.55
410	$ 9.18	$ 8.91	$ 8.63	$ 8.36	$ 8.08	$ 7.81	$ 22.96
420	$ 9.35	$ 9.06	$ 8.78	$ 8.50	$ 8.22	$ 7.94	$ 23.36
430	$ 9.51	$ 9.22	$ 8.94	$ 8.65	$ 8.37	$ 8.08	$ 23.77
440	$ 9.67	$ 9.38	$ 9.09	$ 8.80	$ 8.51	$ 8.22	$ 24.18
450	$ 9.83	$ 9.54	$ 9.24	$ 8.95	$ 8.65	$ 8.36	$ 24.58

Further discounts .... 18% for 1500+ copies, 21% for 2000+, 24% for 2500+, 27% for 3000+, 30% for 4000+

Full colour covers/lamination .... All Trafford prices include full colour covers printed on 10 pt. coated-one-side card stock; lamination is optional at $.50 extra per book (then apply volume discounts).

Inside pages .... Inside pages are printed on 20# white bond. For 60# offset paper (~ 24# bond) or 20# chlorine-free recycled paper, add additional cost of .325¢ per page (.65¢ per sheet).

Spiral or wire comb binding ...... add $.65 to above Total Per Book (then apply volume discounts); add additional $.65 for optional fold-over front flap. Maximum thickness is 520 pages of 20# bond.

Perfect binding thickness .... Maximum thickness is about 700 pages. Minimum thickness is 100 pages (50 sheets) if the cover is laminated, 50 pages (25 sheets) if the cover is non-laminated.

Min./max. dimensions .... Maximum trimmed size for perfect-bound books is 8.25" wide x 10.75" tall – slightly less for thick or laminated books. Minimum dimensions are 5" x 5" (perfect-bound) and 4" x 4" (spiral coil-bound).

Prices subject to change .... Prices are current to March 1, 2003 and are subject to change without notice. They will be adjusted periodically to reflect changes in paper costs and exchange rates.

Minimum retail price .... To allow for appropriate discounts (from 15% to 50%) to libraries, retailers and distributors, and to have an adequate author's royalty, we insist that the retail price be set by the author at a level 2.5 times the single-copy printing cost or higher.

Handling/packaging fee .... When you, as the author, order books for your own distribution, you will pay the price per book indicated above, plus there is a $10.00 fee for handling and packaging materials for orders of fewer than 50 copies.

Colour inserts .... Each page (side) of colour adds $.35 to the print cost, plus there is an inserting fee of $.65 for each ten sheets (or part thereof).

Single-copy Book Printing Cost in Canadian $

Print cost = what you, as author, pay for copies of your own book   Retail price = what a bookstore's customer pays for your book

# of Pages	Single-copy print cost	50 + (-3%)	100 + (-6%)	250+ (-9%)	500+ (-12%)	1000+ (-15%)	Min. Retail Price
50	$ 5.13	$ 4.98	$ 4.82	$ 4.67	$ 4.51	$ 4.36	$ 12.83
100	$ 6.38	$ 6.19	$ 6.00	$ 5.81	$ 5.61	$ 5.42	$ 15.95
110	$ 6.63	$ 6.43	$ 6.23	$ 6.03	$ 5.83	$ 5.64	$ 16.58
120	$ 6.88	$ 6.67	$ 6.47	$ 6.26	$ 6.05	$ 5.85	$ 17.20
130	$ 7.13	$ 6.92	$ 6.70	$ 6.49	$ 6.27	$ 6.06	$ 17.83
140	$ 7.38	$ 7.16	$ 6.94	$ 6.72	$ 6.49	$ 6.27	$ 18.45
150	$ 7.63	$ 7.40	$ 7.17	$ 6.94	$ 6.71	$ 6.49	$ 19.08
160	$ 7.88	$ 7.64	$ 7.41	$ 7.17	$ 6.93	$ 6.70	$ 19.70
170	$ 8.13	$ 7.89	$ 7.64	$ 7.40	$ 7.15	$ 6.91	$ 20.33
180	$ 8.38	$ 8.13	$ 7.88	$ 7.63	$ 7.37	$ 7.12	$ 20.95
190	$ 8.63	$ 8.37	$ 8.11	$ 7.85	$ 7.59	$ 7.34	$ 21.58
200	$ 8.88	$ 8.61	$ 8.35	$ 8.08	$ 7.81	$ 7.55	$ 22.20
210	$ 9.13	$ 8.86	$ 8.58	$ 8.31	$ 8.03	$ 7.76	$ 22.83
220	$ 9.38	$ 9.10	$ 8.82	$ 8.54	$ 8.25	$ 7.97	$ 23.45
230	$ 9.63	$ 9.34	$ 9.05	$ 8.76	$ 8.47	$ 8.19	$ 24.08
240	$ 9.88	$ 9.58	$ 9.29	$ 8.99	$ 8.69	$ 8.40	$ 24.70
250	$ 10.13	$ 9.83	$ 9.52	$ 9.22	$ 8.91	$ 8.61	$ 25.33
260	$ 10.38	$ 10.07	$ 9.76	$ 9.45	$ 9.13	$ 8.82	$ 25.95
270	$ 10.63	$ 10.31	$ 9.99	$ 9.67	$ 9.35	$ 9.04	$ 26.58
280	$ 10.88	$ 10.55	$ 10.23	$ 9.90	$ 9.57	$ 9.25	$ 27.20
290	$ 11.13	$ 10.80	$ 10.46	$ 10.13	$ 9.79	$ 9.46	$ 27.83
300	$ 11.38	$ 11.04	$ 10.70	$ 10.36	$ 10.01	$ 9.67	$ 28.45
310	$ 11.63	$ 11.28	$ 10.93	$ 10.58	$ 10.23	$ 9.89	$ 29.08
320	$ 11.88	$ 11.52	$ 11.17	$ 10.81	$ 10.45	$ 10.10	$ 29.70
330	$ 12.13	$ 11.77	$ 11.40	$ 11.04	$ 10.67	$ 10.31	$ 30.33
340	$ 12.38	$ 12.01	$ 11.64	$ 11.27	$ 10.89	$ 10.52	$ 30.95
350	$ 12.63	$ 12.25	$ 11.87	$ 11.49	$ 11.11	$ 10.74	$ 31.58
360	$ 12.88	$ 12.49	$ 12.11	$ 11.72	$ 11.33	$ 10.95	$ 32.20
370	$ 13.13	$ 12.74	$ 12.34	$ 11.95	$ 11.55	$ 11.16	$ 32.83
380	$ 13.38	$ 12.98	$ 12.58	$ 12.18	$ 11.77	$ 11.37	$ 33.45
390	$ 13.63	$ 13.22	$ 12.81	$ 12.40	$ 11.99	$ 11.59	$ 34.08
400	$ 13.88	$ 13.46	$ 13.05	$ 12.63	$ 12.21	$ 11.80	$ 34.70
410	$ 14.13	$ 13.71	$ 13.28	$ 12.86	$ 12.43	$ 12.01	$ 35.33
420	$ 14.38	$ 13.95	$ 13.52	$ 13.09	$ 12.65	$ 12.22	$ 35.95
430	$ 14.63	$ 14.19	$ 13.75	$ 13.31	$ 12.87	$ 12.44	$ 36.58
440	$ 14.88	$ 14.43	$ 13.99	$ 13.54	$ 13.09	$ 12.65	$ 37.20
450	$ 15.13	$ 14.68	$ 14.22	$ 13.77	$ 13.31	$ 12.86	$ 37.83

Further discounts .... 18% for 1500+ copies, 21% for 2000+, 24% for 2500+, 27% for 3000+, 30% for 4000+

Full colour covers/lamination .... All Trafford prices include full colour covers printed on 10 pt. coated-one-side card stock; lamination is optional at $.75 extra per book (then apply volume discounts).

Inside pages .... Inside pages are printed on 20# white bond. For 60# offset paper (~ 24# bond) or 20# chlorine-free recycled paper, add additional cost of .5¢ per page (one cent per sheet).

Spiral or wire comb binding ...... add $1.00 to above Total Per Book (then apply volume discounts); add additional $1.00 for optional fold-over front flap. Maximum thickness is 520 pages of 20# bond.

Perfect binding thickness .... Maximum thickness is about 700 pages. Minimum thickness is 100 pages (50 sheets) if the cover is laminated, 50 pages (25 sheets) if the cover is non-laminated.

Min./max. dimensions .... Maximum trimmed size for perfect-bound books is 8.25" wide x 10.75" tall – slightly less for thick or laminated books. Minimum sizes are 5" x 5" (perfect-bound) and 4" x 4" (spiral coil-bound).

Prices subject to change .... These prices are current to March 1, 2003 and are subject to change without notice. They will be adjusted periodically to reflect changes in paper costs and other factors.

Minimum retail price .... To allow for appropriate discounts (from 15% to 50%) to libraries, retailers and distributors, and to have an adequate author's royalty, the retail price will be set by the author at a level 2.5 times the single-copy printing cost or higher.

Handling/packaging fee .... When you, as the author, order books for your own distribution, you will pay the price per book indicated above, plus there is a $15.00 fee for handling and packaging materials for orders of fewer than 50 copies.

Colour inserts .... Each page (side) of colour adds $.50 to the print cost, plus there is an inserting fee of $1.00 for each ten sheets (or part thereof).

ISBN 141200000-9

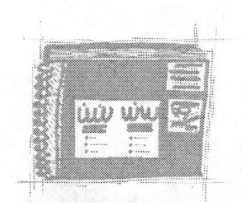

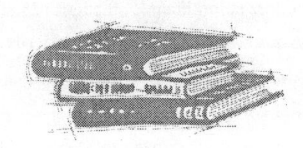

9 781412 000000